PRIMARY
MATHEMATICS

Sara Miller McCune founded SAGE Publishing in 1965 to support the dissemination of usable knowledge and educate a global community. SAGE publishes more than 1000 journals and over 800 new books each year, spanning a wide range of subject areas. Our growing selection of library products includes archives, data, case studies and video. SAGE remains majority owned by our founder and after her lifetime will become owned by a charitable trust that secures the company's continued independence.

Los Angeles | London | New Delhi | Singapore | Washington DC | Melbourne

8th
edition

Claire Mooney, Alice Hansen, Lindsey Davidson,
Sue Fox and Reg Wrathmell

PRIMARY
MATHEMATICS

Knowledge and Understanding

SAGE | LearningMatters

Learning Matters
An imprint of SAGE Publications Ltd
1 Oliver's Yard
55 City Road
London EC1Y 1SP

SAGE Publications Inc.
2455 Teller Road
Thousand Oaks, California 91320

SAGE Publications India Pvt Ltd
B 1/I 1 Mohan Cooperative Industrial Area
Mathura Road
New Delhi 110 044

SAGE Publications Asia-Pacific Pte Ltd
3 Church Street
#10–04 Samsung Hub
Singapore 049483

Editor: Amy Thornton
Production controller: Chris Marke
Project management: Deer Park Productions
Marketing manager: Lorna Patkai
Cover design: Wendy Scott
Typeset by: C&M Digitals (P) Ltd, Chennai, India
Printed in the UK

First published in 2000 by Learning Matters Ltd.
Second edition published in 2002. Third edition
published in 2007. Fourth edition published in 2009.
Fifth edition published in 2011. Sixth edition published
in 2012. Seventh edition published in 2014. Eighth
edition published in 2018.

Library of Congress Control Number: 2017957602

British Library Cataloguing in Publication Data

A catalogue record for this book is available from the
British Library.

ISBN 978-1-5264-4052-5 (pbk)
ISBN 978-1-5264-4051-8

At SAGE we take sustainability seriously. Most of our products are printed in the UK using FSC papers and boards.
When we print overseas we ensure sustainable papers are used as measured by the PREPS grading system.
We undertake an annual audit to monitor our sustainability.

Contents

Contents

About the authors

Lindsey Ferrie (Lindsey Davidson) is currently working as a Consultant Principal in schools across the UK, Europe and globally. She specialises in transformational leadership roles and enjoys the challenge of leading and supporting teachers in challenging circumstances. Lindsey has also worked as an associate inspector for Ofsted in the UK, and regularly inspects schools in other countries. Based in mainland Europe, she regularly runs conferences and workshops for teachers.

Sue Fox has had extensive experience of teaching all ages from Reception to Year 6. She worked as a Senior Mathematics Lecturer in initial teacher training for many years.

Alice Hansen is an educational consultant who has taught in a wide variety of primary schools in England and abroad. She worked for over a decade in Initial Teacher Education (ITE) as a senior lecturer in primary mathematics education at the University of Cumbria before becoming the Programme Leader for the full-time primary Postgraduate Certificate in Education with Qualified Teacher Status. Since becoming an educational consultant she has supported numerous governments, teacher training programmes and schools in England and abroad with curriculum development. She is research active and often teaches in primary schools to keep up-to-date.

Claire Mooney is a Senior Lecturer in Mathematics Education at Trent University in Ontario.

After being the Deputy Head Teacher of a Primary School, Reg Wrathmell's interest in mathematics education took him into a career in Initial Teacher Training. As a Senior Lecturer in Mathematics at The University of Winchester, he taught on both Undergraduate and Postgraduate courses. He was also the mathematics provider for two SCITT courses in Hampshire. Besides developing material for the National Numeracy Strategy, he has been extensively involved in mathematics in-service courses for teachers.

Foreword

Knowing sufficient mathematics and how to teach it well to primary aged children brings with it a number of privileges. You can be the teacher that sets a class on the right road with place value and number sense. You can be that teacher who challenges pupils to quickly grasp a range of applications for mathematics in the real world. You can be delighted when a group who have struggled with an aspect of mathematics start to understand and begin to love mathematics.

We teach in a period where mathematics is a high stakes subject, perhaps the highest stakes subject? It is a period where international competition is as fierce as ever and where international comparative test results and their ranking within the world are seen by some politicians as the only measure of success.

When a country like the United Kingdom decides to leave a trading group and 'go it alone' it brings into stark contrast that countries capacity or perhaps better the capacity of its people to compete in international markets. When there are regions of that country which significantly underperform both educationally and financially, policy makers will turn to schooling and schools who will be expected to be at least part of the solution. Primary school teachers are part of the mathematical capital of a nation, they multiply this several fold with highly effective teaching of mathematics.

When government cabinet members argue for a narrow, restricted mathematics curriculum in the name of 'basics' the profession has to hold firm. We need to train our teachers well and give them the tools with which to enthuse the next generation of pupils making their way through the longest phase of education, the primary years.

This eighth edition of *Achieving QTS Primary Mathematics Knowledge and Understanding* has, for any teacher, the potential to be a very significant contributor to that personal and professional knowledge on which years of excellent practice can be based. There is no doubt that the teachers personal subject knowledge is the first footing which will underpin confidence, communication and a developing subject pedagogy which can be fine tuned to suit the increasing range of learners encountered by primary teachers today. This experienced writing team have developed a turn of the written and diagrammatically phrase which makes mathematics comprehensible to the reader. They model the important clarity and forms of explanation which can be directly transferred to the classroom.

The reader is introduced to, and 'coached' towards; important principles which research and experience have shown are effective in mathematics education. An example is talk. Talking is introduced in the opening chapter but which can be heard on every page of the book where the book's voice talks the reader systematically through all those aspects covered by the English Primary National Curriculum. Language develops in the various chapters of this book as of course it should. Mathematics is a language of its own, it is an international language.

Throughout the book summaries and reflective tasks strengthen a narrative of mathematics and mathematics education through a guided exploration of some basic, some more challenging, and for some, puzzling parts of mathematics. These experienced teacher educator authors know which parts of mathematics challenge both children and those new to teaching. Questions are posed by the writing team such as, why do children struggle with fractions? A short summary expands on and answers the question. From there we are introduced to the fantastic world of fractions. The authors carefully introduce the reader to ideas and talk the reader through examples.

In mathematics lessons much good practice is underpinned when learners have the opportunity to say, "this is how I did it". Mooney, Hansen, Ferrie, Fox and Wrathmell systematically tell us how they 'do' these calculations. We see the working in algorithms and diagrams and we are given examples, which prove a rule and others which fall short of proof. This ensures that this book offers practical advice for teachers to use with immediate effect.

When you are seven years old your primary teacher is often the most capable mathematician you know. Certainly the teacher should be the most capable mathematics educator in the child's life at that point, the work of the authors in this book can enable all primary teachers to attain that accolade.

Alison Borthwick, Mathematics Consultant, Researcher and Author

Alan Cross, Manchester Institute of Education, University of Manchester

1

Introduction

Introduction

About this book

This book has been written to cater for the needs of primary trainees on all courses of initial teacher training in England and other parts of the UK. By the end of your course, you will be required to demonstrate your subject knowledge and understanding and your competence in using this knowledge in your teaching. A secure subject knowledge of mathematics is required for the award of Qualified Teacher Status (QTS) or its equivalent. This book will also be useful to newly qualified teachers (NQTs) and other professionals working in education who have identified aspects of their mathematics subject knowledge which require attention.

This book has been written with the Teachers' Standards firmly at its core. The Teachers' Standards in England (DfE, 2011c) came into force from 1 September 2012. They define the minimum level of practice expected of all teachers from the point of being awarded QTS.

There have been many changes in education in the last few years. Following the Tickell Report (Tickell, 2011), changes to the Early Years Foundation Stage (EYFS) were implemented, including a new Statutory Framework for the Early Years Foundation Stage, mandatory from September 2012 and updated in 2014. That led to the new National Curriculum in England, which maintained schools in England are legally required to follow. This book includes information on the programmes of study for National Curriculum mathematics and on the mathematics Early Learning Goals for children in the Early Years.

Features of the main chapters of this book include:

- clear links with the Teachers' Standards;
- information about the curriculum context, including the mathematics National Curriculum in England and the Statutory Framework for the Early Years Foundation Stage;
- mathematics knowledge and understanding;

- reflective and practical activities for you to undertake, many of which are related to pedagogy;
- research summaries that give additional background insights into how children's understanding of mathematical concepts develops;
- a summary of key learning points;
- suggestions for further reading on the aspect in question.

There are also self-assessment questions so that you can check on how well you have assimilated the knowledge and understanding. The answers to these questions are contained in a separate chapter. The book also contains a glossary of terms, and details of publications referenced in the main chapters.

A mathematics subject knowledge really does matter!

A healthy subject knowledge of mathematics is widely acknowledged as a critical factor in the complex process of teaching mathematics itself (Ball and Bass, 2000; Morris, 2001; Rowland et al., 2001; TDA, 2007). Few nowadays would argue that planning, teaching and assessing mathematics lessons, setting learning outcomes, choosing appropriate activities and resources, identifying children's errors and misconceptions, asking and responding to questions, and so on, could be achieved without a sound knowledge of mathematics in the first place. Within primary schools currently there is a clear drive to raise standards in mathematics through raising expectations and national target setting.

Implicit within this drive to raise standards in mathematics is the requirement for teachers to have the necessary subject knowledge to teach confidently and effectively. Ma (1999) proposed that a *profound understanding of fundamental mathematics* (PUFM) is crucial to effective mathematics teaching. PUFM refers to the depth, breadth and thoroughness of the knowledge that is required to be an accomplished teacher of primary mathematics. Ma suggested that teachers with PUFM make connections between mathematical concepts and procedures from the simple to the complex, appreciate different facets of an idea and various approaches to a solution, are particularly aware of the simple but powerful foundational concepts and principles of mathematics, and are knowledgeable about the whole primary mathematics curriculum, not just the content of a particular age level. This may well seem like a large a burden. However, persisting with the development of an appropriate level of mathematics subject knowledge will ensure confident mathematics teaching that motivates, challenges and extends the children.

The importance of talking mathematics

As well as securing confidence in your subject knowledge of mathematics, you need to be ready to talk mathematics. Increasingly, teachers are seeing the benefits of talking about mathematics with children from a young age. This is a stepping stone to confident use of mathematical language later on. The following Research Summary outlines some of the theory behind this:

RESEARCH SUMMARY

In the *Independent Review of Mathematics Teaching in Early Years Settings and Primary Schools*, Sir Peter Williams offered a number of recommendations for the long term to enhance the standing of the teaching profession and the mathematical learning of the children in their care (Williams, 2008, page 4). One of the issues raised was the need for high-quality talk in mathematics. Williams explains why the vitally important question of the classroom discussion of mathematics is an issue he singles out. He states, it is often suggested that *mathematics itself is a language* but it must not be overlooked that only by constructive dialogue in the medium of the English language in the classroom can logic and reasoning be fully developed – the factors at the very heart of embedded learning in mathematics (Williams, 2008, page 4).

Neil Mercer and his colleagues have undertaken research that tries to address the issues surrounding mathematical talk in primary classrooms and early years settings. They identified that:

- the teacher has a key role in enabling children to talk and reason together effectively;
- providing children with guidance and practice in how to use language for reasoning enables them to use it more effectively as a tool for working on mathematics problems together;
- improving the quality of children's use of language improves individuals' learning also;
- the teacher is an important model and guide for children's use of language and reasoning (Littleton et al., 2005; Mercer and Sams, 2006a, 2006b).

The importance of reasoning for the development of your own mathematical knowledge

The development of your own mathematical reasoning skills has an impact not only on your own mathematical knowledge but also on the quality of your teaching.

RESEARCH FOCUS

Mathematical explanations

Charalambous et al. (2011) have written extensively about the development of teachers' mathematical explanations during the period of their teacher training. They followed a small group of pre-service teachers through their training, monitored the development of their mathematical explanations and explored the reasons for this development. The pre-service teachers' explanations at the beginning of their course were limited and tended to focus on how to carry out mathematical procedures, often reflecting the ways that they were taught themselves.

The teachers in the study progressed at very different rates in terms of their ability to give mathematical explanations. Those teachers who made the greatest gains in the quality of their explanations were those who, among other things, were able to develop their own ability to reason mathematically and to reconsider and refine their own ideas about what it means to reason mathematically. They said that being able to explain their ideas and thinking in a logical way was essential to improving their mathematical explanations.

What do we mean by 'reasoning skills' and how do you develop them?

The Advisory Committee on Mathematics Education's (ACME) response to the draft National Curriculum called for a clear definition of mathematical reasoning and suggested the following:

Mathematical reasoning requires analysing information presented in different forms, recognising given information, identifying what additional information is needed and what forms of reasoning can provide it; identifying and conjecturing patterns, relationships, and generalisations; testing, inducing, deducing, and proving; and communicating ideas in mathematical language. (ACME, 2012, p.5)

Although there is not one clear definition, it is clear that 'reasoning' skills include the following:

- The ability to make sense of mathematics, not just the ability to follow prescribed rules and procedures.
- The ability to know which mathematical procedure to apply to a problem, not just the ability to 'do' the procedure.
- The ability to estimate and discuss a likely result before completing any advanced calculations, not just the ability to find the answer.
- The ability to check your answers, via other methods, to ensure your calculations are correct, not just a need to be told that your answer is correct.

Marcus Witt (2014) offers an explanation of reasoning through an example of reasoning in the classroom:

EXAMPLE

In Joyce's room, the children are solving a puzzle which looks like the one below.

★	★	★	★	8
£	$	&	♣	17
★	♠	★	♠	16
$	★	€	♣	11
9	11	14	18	

The discussion centred on the ways in which the children had solved the puzzle:

Joyce: How did you start the puzzle?

Anish: I saw that the top row was all stars. There are four stars and together they come to 8, so I knew that the star must be worth 2.

Joyce:	(Feigning not to understand fully) So, explain to me exactly how you knew each one was worth 2.
Anish:	Well, there are four stars. The whole row comes to 8, so I knew that four stars equals 8, so each star must be worth 2. See 2 and 2 more is 4 and 2 more is 6 and 2 more makes 8.
Joyce:	Fantastic, good strategy. Thank you for explaining that to me so clearly. Can someone else explain how they went on from there?
Sam:	Once you know what the star is worth, you can find out the other symbols.
Joyce:	Good thought. Can you give us an example of how you worked out one of the other symbols?
Sam:	Well, it's hard to explain. In the bit where you have two stars and two spades, you can add the two stars together to get 4. As they all come to 16, you know that the spade must be worth 6.
Joyce:	I'm not sure I followed what you said at the end. How did you know that the spade must be worth 5?
Sam:	It's easy, miss. The two spades must be worth 12 all together, because the two stars are worth 4 and the total is 16. If the two spades are worth 10, then each one must be worth 6.
Joyce:	Fantastic, now I've got it. Does anybody want to ask Sam about how he got 6?
Kim:	Now it's easy. Once you know a couple of the symbols, you can find out the others.
Joyce:	Can you give us an example of another symbol that you found out?
Kim:	Easy. In the column with two stars, a spade and the dollar, you only have to find out the dollar thing. You know all the others.

This discussion is less about the different calculation strategies and more about the problem-solving strategies that the children are using. The children are still using and applying a number of different mental mathematics strategies.

The vocabulary of reasoning

Marcus Witt (2014) also explores some key words associated with mathematical reasoning. Use of these words in discussions of mathematics can be a sign that reasoning is being used. This is useful when teaching (as children's use of these words is a sign of their learning) but can also be useful for you when developing your own undersanding.

Suggested key words and phrases to prompt reasoning

Question (key words in italics)	Answer (key words in italics)
How did you know that the answer was 45?	I knew *because* 20 and 20 is 40, *so* 20 and 25 must be 40 and 5 more.
Why do you think the answer will be an even number?	*I think* it will be even *because* an even number added to an even number *always* makes an even number.
What made you so sure that the shape couldn't be a square?	*If* the shape was a square, *then* it would have to have only right angles. *As* that corner isn't a right angle, the shape can't be a square.
Can you explain why you added one back?	*If* you are trying to take away 9, but you have actually taken away 10, *then* you've taken away too much, *so* you have to give one back.
Tell us how you knew it would be more than 10.	*Whenever* you add two numbers together, unless one's a minus number, they *will always make* a bigger number. *So* 10 and something *will always be* bigger than 10.
What do you think will happen when we add 10 to this number? *Why?*	*I think that* the digit in the middle column will go up by one, but the others won't change, *because* we are only adding a 10, so only the tens column will change.
Is it always true that adding 10 will only change the tens digit.	It's not always true, because sometimes, *if* the tens digit is already a 9, *then* the tens digit will go to zero and the hundreds digit will go up by one.
Is it possible for a fraction to have a bigger number on the top than the bottom? *How?*	*It is possible, because* sometimes a fraction is more than one, like 5 quarters, *so therefore* you would have to write the 5 first and then out of 4.
What makes you think these are a group?	All those are a group *because* they all end in a 5, or a 0. *But*, actually, those others could be a different group *because* they are all less than 12.

The language of mathematical reasoning will become more familiar to you as you begin to consolidate your learning and start working with children. It is important to be aware of the importance of reasoning as you begin your training and to be mindful of the ways you can develop your reasoning skills.

The Teachers' Standards

This book refers mostly to the mathematics-related subject standards you will be required to demonstrate in order to be awarded QTS. (See Mooney et al., 2018 for pedagogical and professional theory and practice.) This explicitly fulfils the following Standards:

A teacher must:

3. Demonstrate good subject and curriculum knowledge

- have a secure knowledge of the relevant subject(s) and curriculum areas, foster and maintain pupils' interest in the subject, and address misunderstandings

- demonstrate a critical understanding of developments in the subject and curriculum areas, and promote the value of scholarship

4. **Plan and teach well structured lessons**
   - impart knowledge and develop understanding through effective use of lesson time
   - promote a love of learning and children's intellectual curiosity
   - contribute to the design and provision of an engaging curriculum within the relevant subject area(s)

8. **Fulfil wider professional responsibilities**
   - take responsibility for improving teaching through appropriate professional development

In addition to these obvious standards, by having a secure subject knowledge you will also be able to support your work in meeting many of the other standards that involve giving appropriate feedback to children, planning for progression, etc.

This book covers the full range of the primary mathematics curriculum but also goes beyond to look at further aspects. The consideration given to mathematical language, and reasoning and proof should ensure you are able to make the connections between mathematical concepts and go some way towards gaining the profound understanding mentioned earlier.

Curriculum context

We have focused in this book on the core areas of mathematics subject knowledge and understanding that you will need to develop the mathematical knowledge and understanding of the children you work with.

A closer look at the Purpose of Study of the National Curriculum for mathematics is useful here as an introduction to the kind of knowledge required to 'teach' children.

Purpose of study

Mathematics is a creative and highly interconnected discipline that has been developed over centuries, providing the solution to some of history's most intriguing problems. It is essential to everyday life, critical to science, technology and engineering, and necessary for financial literacy and most forms of employment. A high-quality mathematics education therefore provides a foundation for understanding the world, the ability to reason mathematically, an appreciation of the beauty and power of mathematics, and a sense of enjoyment and curiosity about the subject. (DfE 2013b, page 3)

Understanding the context of the curriculum helps you to make sense of how your children have been taught and why. Therefore, in each chapter we have included context about the primary National Curriculum programmes of study and the Early Learning Goals for children in the Early Years Foundation Stage in mathematics.

The Early Years Foundation Stage

The Statutory Framework for the Early Years Foundation Stage (EYFS) sets the standards that all early years providers must meet to ensure that children learn and develop well and are kept healthy and safe. It promotes teaching and learning to ensure children's 'school readiness' and gives children the broad range of knowledge and skills that provide the right foundation for good future progress through school and life. Children will remain in the EYFS until the end of the academic year in which they turn five years of age. In practice this will mean that children will follow EYFS until they finish their Reception year.

There are seven areas of learning and development that shape the educational programmes in early years settings. The three *prime* areas are:

- communication and language;
- physical development; and
- personal, social and emotional development.

The four *specific* areas are:

- literacy;
- mathematics;
- understanding the world; and
- expressive arts and design.

For the purposes of this book we shall focus on these, specifically the area of learning and development in 'mathematics', which *involves providing children with opportunities to develop and improve their skills in counting, understanding and using numbers, calculating simple addition and subtraction problems; and to describe shapes, spaces, and measure* (DfE, 2017a, page 8). Crucially, the focus in mathematics is that children talk about and apply mathematics in a way that makes common sense to them (Tickell, 2011, page 103).

Mathematics in the National Curriculum

The primary National Curriculum for mathematics is split into three key stages: Key Stage 1 (5–7 years), Lower Key Stage 2 (7–9 years) and Upper Key Stage 2 (9–11 years). Each key stage includes attainment targets, which state what pupils are expected to know, apply and understand of the matters, skills and processes specified in the mathematics programme of study. The mathematics National Curriculum in England has three aims to ensure that all pupils:

- become **fluent** in the fundamentals of mathematics, including through varied and frequent practice with increasingly complex problems over time, so that pupils develop conceptual understanding and the ability to recall and apply knowledge rapidly and accurately;
- **reason mathematically** by following a line of enquiry, conjecturing relationships and generalisations, and developing an argument, justification or proof using mathematical language;
- can **solve problems** by applying their mathematics to a variety of routine and non-routine problems with increasing sophistication, including breaking down problems into a series of simpler steps and persevering in seeking solutions.

Furthermore, the National Curriculum explains how:

Mathematics is an interconnected subject in which pupils need to be able to move fluently between representations of mathematical ideas. The programmes of study are, by necessity, organised into apparently distinct domains, but pupils should make rich connections across mathematical ideas to develop fluency, mathematical reasoning and competence in solving increasingly sophisticated problems. They should also apply their mathematical knowledge to science and other subjects. (DfE 2013b, page 3)

In order to support children with this, you need a good subject knowledge to see the connections, spot patterns, be fluent, reason mathematically and solve problems yourself.

Assessment of primary mathematics

In England, all schools can develop and deploy their own approaches to formative assessment to support pupil attainment and progression. Each school's assessment framework should be built into their school curriculum, so that schools can check what children have learned and whether they are on track to meet expectations at the end of the key stage, and so that they can report regularly to parents.

At the time of writing, the DfE have recently confirmed that the external testing for mathematics will continue at the end of Key Stage 2. In the Government's response (DfE, 2011b) to the Bew Review (2011) into Key Stage 2 testing, assessment and accountability they stated:

> It is important that mathematics tests are accessible to all pupils and do not unfairly disadvantage weaker readers. At the time of publication, The Standards and Testing Agency was reviewing all future National Curriculum Tests in mathematics to ensure that they remain accessible to all pupils, and that they are primarily tests of mathematics rather than reading. (DfE, 2011b: 10)

In September 2017, the Department for Education published the *Primary Assessment in England Government Consultation Response*. This document outlines the government response to the consultation on the long-term future of primary assessment that ran from March 2017 to June 2017. This consultation

> sought views on a number of key proposals about the future of the statutory primary assessment system. These included assessment in the early years, the starting point for measuring the progress that pupils make at primary school, statutory end-of-key stage teacher assessment and proposals to ensure that we have a proportionate assessment system. (DfE, 2017b, page 4)

The document gives details of the government's aim to

> remove the statutory requirement for schools to report teacher assessment judgements in English reading and mathematics at the end of key stage 2 from the 2018 to 2019 academic year onwards, once the relevant legislation has been amended. We believe that removing this duty to report judgements against the statutory teacher assessment frameworks will reduce burdens for teachers. (DfEb, 2017, pages 24–5)

It makes clear, however, that schools' statutory requirement to report pupils' attainment and progress to parents will remain.

Also outlined is the government's plan to

> make assessments at the end of key stage 1 (both national curriculum tests and statutory teacher assessment) non-statutory as soon as the reception baseline assessment has become fully established. If possible, we intend to make this change from the 2022 to 2023 academic year onwards. (DfE, 2017b, page 20)

Finally, the document explains clear plans to introduce the Multiplication Tables Check (a statutory test announced in 2016) at the end of Year 4.

The Primary Framework for Literacy and Mathematics

While it was not statutory, the Primary Framework for Mathematics contained guidance and resources to help teachers to plan and teach mathematics to 3–11-year-old children. Many schools used the framework in their planning because by doing so they were meeting the requirements of the National Curriculum at the time.

There were seven strands in the Framework for Mathematics. These included:

- using and applying mathematics;
- counting and understanding number;
- knowing and using number facts;
- calculating;
- understanding shape;
- measuring;
- handling data.

The framework encouraged a planning and teaching style for Key Stages 1 and 2 that used 'blocks'. These required teachers to consider links between different strands. This revised approach to teaching mathematics not only included the opportunity for teachers to be more creative in their approach to teaching, it also required them to have a secure subject knowledge.

Although the requirement to have regard for the primary national strategies has been discontinued, you may find that schools and individual teachers you work with are still using whole blocks or adapted units of this framework in their medium-term and long-term planning for mathematics, or other elements, such as the three-part numeracy lesson.

Outcomes

This book can be used to start to address the development of your mathematical subject knowledge. Through developing subject knowledge of mathematics, including patterns and relationships, the ability to communicate, discuss, generalise, hypothesise and relate mathematics to the wider world, you will develop positive and active attitudes towards and greater enthusiasm for mathematics. It should also stimulate a sense of curiosity and enjoyment and encourage communication of these positive attitudes to children, resulting in teaching that is effective, challenging and extremely rewarding.

By using this book to support your own subject knowledge development, you will be able to learn the knowledge and develop the understanding required to teach primary mathematics, and the appropriate elements of 'Problem solving, reasoning and numeracy' in the EYFS.

So that you can check on how well you have assimilated the subject knowledge and test your understanding, you may wish to try the self-assessment questions related to each aspect that we address. You will find these in a separate chapter towards the end of the book. The answers to these questions are provided for you in a separate section.

For those undertaking credits for a Master's Degree, we have included suggestions for further work and extended study at the end of each chapter in a section called 'M-Level Extension'.

FURTHER READING

To support you in understanding the curriculum context, you may find it helpful to refer to some of the following documentation:

DfE (2013) *Mathematics Programmes of Study: Key Stages 1 and 2. National Curriculum in England*. London: DfE. Available at https://www.gov.uk/government/uploads/system/uploads/attachment_data/file/239129/PRIMARY_National_Curriculum_-_Mathematics.pdf

DfE (2017) *Statutory Framework for the Early Years Foundation Stage: Setting the Standards for Learning, Development and Care for Children from Birth to Five*. London: DfE. Available at https://www.gov.uk/government/publications/early-years-foundation-stage-framework--2

Ofsted (2007) *Mathematics: Understanding the Score – Improving Practice in Mathematics Teaching at Primary Level*. London: Ofsted.

2

Number: place value, addition, subtraction, multiplication and division

Teachers' Standards

A teacher must:

3. Demonstrate good subject and curriculum knowledge

    - have a secure knowledge of the relevant subject(s) and curriculum areas, foster and maintain pupils' interest in the subject, and address misunderstandings
    - demonstrate a critical understanding of developments in the subject and curriculum areas, and promote the value of scholarship

4. Plan and teach well structured lessons

    - impart knowledge and develop understanding through effective use of lesson time
    - promote a love of learning and children's intellectual curiosity
    - contribute to the design and provision of an engaging curriculum within the relevant subject area(s)

8. Fulfil wider professional responsibilities

    - take responsibility for improving teaching through appropriate professional development

Curriculum context

Early Years Foundation Stage

The Early Years Foundation Stage recognises the importance of certain key skills in mathematical development. These include counting and working with numbers. The mathematical understanding of the children should be developed through games, songs, stories and play to encourage experimenting with numbers, including those larger than 10.

National Curriculum programmes of study

Within the Mathematics National Curriculum, the Number Programme of Study states the knowledge, skills and understanding which are to be taught throughout Key Stages 1 and 2.

At Key Stage 1, the principal focus of mathematics teaching is to ensure that children develop confidence and mental fluency with whole numbers, counting and place value. This involves working with numerals, words and the four operations, including with practical resources. During Lower Key Stage 2, the principal focus of mathematics teaching is to ensure that children become increasingly fluent with whole numbers and the four operations, including number facts and the concept of place value. Children will develop efficient written and mental methods and perform calculations accurately with increasingly large whole numbers. They will also develop their ability to solve a range of problems, including with simple fractions and decimal place value.

During Upper Key Stage 2, the principal focus of mathematics teaching is to ensure that children extend their understanding of the number system and place value to include larger integers. This should develop the connections that pupils make between multiplication and division with fractions, decimals, percentages and ratio. Children will develop their ability to solve a wider range of problems, including increasingly complex properties of numbers and arithmetic, and problems demanding efficient written and mental methods of calculation.

Number: place value, addition, subtraction, multiplication and division

Introduction

For thousands of years people have used numbers to keep records, to investigate, to solve problems and to predict. These uses often had very concrete applications: for example, recording crop yields at harvest. As the use of number became more complex, formal operations were used. These form the basis of arithmetic (from the Greek *arithmetike* – the art of numbers). When Pythagoras (582–507 BCE) founded the Pythagorean Brotherhood it became, in effect, a religious community and one of the things it worshipped was Number. From the ancient Egyptians, the Greeks and the Babylonians to the present day, number has formed an intrinsic part of daily life. Spend 24 hours noting all the times you encounter numbers in any context and you will be truly amazed at just how numerate we need to be to function effectively within society today.

For more information on the Pythagorean Brotherhood, see the section on Pythagoras' theorem, in Chapter 7.

This chapter addresses the structural laws underpinning arithmetic. It outlines a range of algorithms for tackling the four rules of number.

RESEARCH SUMMARY

Gray and Tall (2001) distinguished between the processes in mathematics and the procedures. They believe that processes do not include any implication that they are carried out in a unique manner. For example, the 'process of addition' might use counting on or a formal written algorithm, but which method is not implied in the process. Conversely 'procedure' describes a specific algorithm. Children who interpret processes only as procedures make mathematics harder for themselves. Children who do not restrict their understanding of processes to procedures, see processes as flexible procepts. The divergence between the two is referred to as the 'proceptual divide'. Gray and Tall argue that the difference between success and failure lies in the difference between the use of procepts and procedures.

Anghileri (2006) stressed the importance of understanding appropriate language prior to tackling multiplication and division. This was revealed in research using sticks made up of differently coloured cubes. For example, using sticks 8 cubes long, with 2 cubes of each colour, the children were asked to identify how many colours there were. For many of the children, the 'how many' led them to count all, i.e. 8. They were then asked to make a pattern stick using 5 different colours with 3 of each colour. A common error was producing a stick with 5 cubes of different colours and 3 further cubes. There was a difficulty in identifying the roles of the numbers 3 and 5 and also of the term 'each'. 'Each' is fundamentally important to understanding multiplication and division.

Place value

In order to understand number and tackle standard written algorithms it is important to have a very clear understanding of place value. Place value is used by number systems that allow the same digit to carry different values based on its position, i.e. the place has a particular value. We use the Hindu-Arabic base 10 number system. The ancient Egyptians also used a base 10 system but they did not have a place value concept. The earliest known example of a place value system was that of the Babylonians. They worked in bases 60 and 360. We still use bases 60 and 360 in some areas ourselves, e.g. 360 degrees in a complete turn and 60 seconds in a minute, 60 minutes in an hour.

REFLECTIVE TASK

Consider the number 3,246,018. What number is it? How did you know?

You will have used your knowledge of place value to work out that this number was three million, two hundred and forty-six thousand and eighteen. For example, you might have done this quickly by grouping the digits into sets of threes and knowing that a number with six digits behind it is a million. We can also use similar place value ideas with decimal numbers; this is discussed later in the chapter.

See the section on decimals, in Chapter 3, to consider how this table relates to multiplying and dividing by powers of ten.

We need to be aware that the same digit represents a different number depending on which place it occupies (its **column value**). For example, every time a digit moves a place to the left, it becomes ten times bigger. Similarly, when a digit moves one place to the right, it becomes ten times smaller. This can be demonstrated below:

$$
\begin{aligned}
1000 &= 10^3 \\
100 &= 10^2 \\
10 &= 10^1 \\
1 &= 10^0 \\
0.1 &= 10^{-1} \\
0.01 &= 10^{-2} \\
0.001 &= 10^{-3} \\
0.0001 &= 10^{-4}
\end{aligned}
$$

This table uses standard form. See the section on this in Chapter 3.

PRACTICAL TASK

Create a concept map of what you know about the number 26. The diagram below is a starting point:

20 + 6

26

2 tens and 6 ones (or units)

4 ones (or units)
less than thirty

one more than half of 50

Our place value number system has certain principles.

- The idea of treating a group of objects as a unit, so ten ones can be one unit of ten, and ten tens can be one unit of a hundred.
- Using the same symbols repeatedly so all numbers can be represented using the 10 digits: 0, 1, 2, 3, 4, 5, 6, 7, 8 and 9.
- The position of the digit relative to any other digits in the number determines its value (column value); the larger groupings are always on the left. (Quantity value is the value you assign to a digit when you have established its value from its position in the number. For example, in 372 its column tells you that the value of the 7 is greater than the 2 and fewer than the 3. Knowing that the 7 is in the 'tens' column can then help you to assign it a 'quantity value' of 70.)
- To identify the size of the number you need to work out the value of each of the digits and then add them, e.g. in 358, the 3 represents 300, the 5 represents 50 and the 8 is 8 ones. The total value of the whole number is the sum of these values, $300 + 50 + 8 = 358$.

The role of 0 (zero) as a 'place holder' is crucial. When 2 is multiplied by 10, the answer is 20. There are now 2 tens instead of 2 units. The zero is holding the place for the units to show that the units column is empty. *Zero* comes from the Latin *zephirum*, which means empty or blank. The symbol 0 originated in India. Al-Khwarizmi explained the Indian number system in 830 CE, but it took a further 400 years before zero was used in western number systems.

For more information on al-Khwarizmi, see the start of Chapter 5.

RESEARCH SUMMARY

Thompson (2009) and Thompson and Bramald (2002) provide a more detailed discussion of the 'column value' and 'quantity value' aspects of place value. They also consider historical perspectives in terms of the ways that young children have traditionally been introduced to place value and how this relates to the development of mental and written calculation skills.

(Continued)

(Continued)

They argue that the traditional definition of place value, which would explain the number 43 as '4 in the tens column' or '4 lots of 10', is an outdated one and does not reflect the way that children actually carry out mental calculations. So, for example, when adding 43 and 52, most people would think in terms of '40 plus 50' and '3 plus 2', that is, 'quantity value' rather than 'column value'. Thompson and Bramald provide similar examples involving subtraction, multiplication and division, and also demonstrate how 'quantity value' underpins informal pencil and paper arithmetic. It is only the traditional pencil and paper methods that utilise 'column value'.

The four rules of number

The four rules of number are addition, subtraction, multiplication and division. There are various relationships between these rules. Addition can be viewed as the **inverse** of subtraction and subtraction as the **inverse** of addition. Equally multiplication and division can be seen as **inverse** operations. Multiplication can be tackled as repeated addition and division as repeated subtraction. There is a range of methods for solving problems involving each of these operations.

Addition

It is important to recognise that many addition problems can be solved quickly and efficiently using mental methods. Many mental strategies involve working left-to-right, i.e. largest columns first. For example, adding 234 and 325 mentally could give rise to the following steps:

Two hundred add three hundred gives five hundred. Thirty add twenty gives fifty, and four add five is nine. So it is five hundred and fifty-nine.

The expanded written method

This method allows for an informal pencil and paper calculation, which builds on the mental strategies already discussed.

To tackle a problem such as 324 + 438 it is first necessary to write the question vertically:

```
  324
+ 438
─────
  700  (add the hundreds first)
   50  (add the tens next)
   12  (then add the units)
─────
  762  (finally add mentally from top to bottom or bottom to top)
```

This method can be used whatever the size of the numbers. For example, 2468 + 1357:

```
  2468
+ 1357
──────
  3000
   700
   110
    15
──────
  3825
```

A standard algorithm

The standard written algorithm for addition can be viewed as shorthand notation for this expanded method. Looking at this example again using the standard algorithm gives:

```
  2468
+ 1357
──────
  3825
   1 1
```

represents the 100 in 60 + 50 = 110 represents the 10 in 8 + 7 = 15

Subtraction

As with addition, there are many effective and efficient strategies for tackling subtraction problems mentally. The first example of a written method below draws on one such example, that of 'counting on' or complementary addition.

Complementary addition

This method builds on the mental method which frequently involves the visual image of an empty number line. To answer the question 84 – 46, the difference is found by counting on from the smaller to the larger number in steps along the number line:

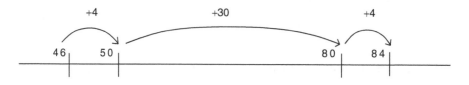

Hence, the answer to 84 – 46 is 4 + 30 + 4 which is 38.

This method can be extended in written form, giving an informal pencil and paper method for complementary addition. Using the above example gives:

$$\begin{array}{r} 84 \\ -46 \\ \hline 4 \;\; \text{(to 50)} \\ 30 \;\; \text{(to 80)} \\ 4 \;\; \text{(to 84)} \\ \hline 38 \end{array}$$

This method can be applied equally effectively to larger numbers. For example, 5356 – 1583:

$$\begin{array}{r} 5356 \\ -1583 \\ \hline 17 \;\; \text{(to 1600)} \\ 400 \;\; \text{(to 2000)} \\ 3356 \;\; \text{(to 5356)} \\ \hline 3000 \\ 700 \\ 60 \\ 13 \\ \hline 3773 \end{array} \qquad or \qquad \begin{array}{r} 5356 \\ -1583 \\ \hline 17 \\ 400 \\ 3356 \\ \hline 3773 \\ \scriptstyle 1 \end{array}$$

Decomposition
This method is the one that is frequently taught as the standard algorithm for subtraction. It involves regrouping numbers to support the calculation. For example, 143 – 27:

Hundreds	Tens	Units
1	3	13
	2	7
1	1	6

Written in the conventional way this gives:

$$\begin{array}{r} 1\overset{3}{4}\overset{1}{3} \\ -\ 27 \\ \hline 116 \end{array}$$

This method works for any numbers. Looking at the last example given for the complementary addition method, 5356 – 1583, gives:

$$\begin{array}{r} \overset{4}{5}\overset{12}{3}\overset{1}{5}6 \\ -\ 1583 \\ \hline 3773 \end{array}$$

This method involves keeping the overall value of the **minuend** the same throughout the calculation. The **minuend** is the number from which something is being subtracted. The **subtrahend** is the number subtracted.

Equal addition
This method of subtraction involves changing the value of both the minuend and subtrahend by the same amount. It is based on the fact that, if the same number is added to both, the difference remains unchanged. This was taught as the 'borrow and pay back' method of subtraction in schools in the earlier parts of the twentieth century.

Looking at the first example in decomposition, 143 – 27, the equal addition method gives:

10 is added to the minuend

$1\ 4\ ^1 3$

$-^{1}2\ 7$

$1\ 6$

10 is added to the subtrahend to ensure the difference is unchanged

Areas of potential confusion lie in the language of 'borrow', the obvious question being 'where from?' One way of traditionally setting out these questions can also give rise to difficulty. For example, the 10 being added to the units in the minuend is represented in the same way as the 10 being added to the tens column in the subtrahend. However, these tens are treated differently in the calculation. So, $^1 3$ in the minuend represents $^1 2$ units but $^1 2$ in the subtrahend represents 3 tens and not 12 as suggested by the representation in the minuend.

These potential confusions aside, this method offers an effective way of undertaking these calculations that is closely linked to balancing equations within algebra.

PRACTICAL TASK

Consider the final example from decomposition, 5356 – 1583, and try to answer the question using the equal addition method.

$$\begin{array}{r} {\scriptstyle 1\ \ 1} \\ 5356 \\ -^1 1^1 583 \\ \hline 3773 \end{array}$$

Multiplication

As already seen with addition and subtraction, there is a wide range of strategies that can be used to multiply numbers. This chapter will consider some of the informal written methods, which are frequently derived from mental methods. It will also outline some more standard methods of multiplying using pencil and paper calculations.

Repeated addition
One of the earliest methods of multiplying involves knowledge of the relation-ship between addition and multiplication. Once it is realised that multiplication can be seen as repeated addition, then this fact can be used to solve simple multi-plication problems. For example, 6×4:

This can be calculated as $4 + 4 + 4 + 4 + 4 + 4 = 24$

It can quickly be seen that this method is rather limited and would be very cum-bersome for large calculations. However, knowledge of multiplication by 10, 100, 1000, etc. can be used along with repeated addition to extend this method. For example, 354×232:

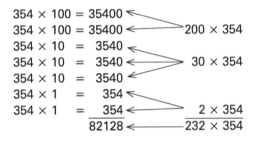

A standard algorithm
The standard algorithm frequently taught is dependent on the **distributive law**. This means that a question such as 24×35 is actually tackled as $(24 \times 30) + (24 \times 5)$:

For more information on the distributive law, see the section later in this chapter.

$$
\begin{array}{r}
2\,4 \\
\times \quad 3\,5 \\
\hline
1\,2{}_2 0 \\
7{}_1 2\,0 \\
\hline
8\,4\,0 \\
\end{array}
\quad
\begin{array}{l}
(5 \times 24) \\
(30 \times 24) \\
(35 \times 24)
\end{array}
$$

To see what is happening it is possible to write this in an expanded form:

$$24$$
$$\times\ 35$$
$$\overline{20} \rightarrow\ 5\times4$$
$$100 \rightarrow\ 5\times20$$
$$120 \rightarrow 30\times4$$
$$600 \rightarrow 30\times20$$
$$\overline{840} \rightarrow 35\times24$$

The standard algorithm is a shorthand version of the above form.

A tabular method

Another way of tackling multiplication, which illustrates how it is underpinned by the distributive law, involves a tabular form of calculation. For example, taking the example of 24 × 35 above:

×	30	5	
20	600	100	700
4	120	20	140
			840

This is a very useful method as it makes explicit how the distributive law applies to multiplication.

Gelosia multiplication

This method of multiplication dates back to twelfth-century India. It is also sometimes called 'Chinese' multiplication, 'lattice' multiplication or 'grating' multiplication. This method depends on producing a grid so that place value is implicit within the structure. Take the above example of 35 × 24:

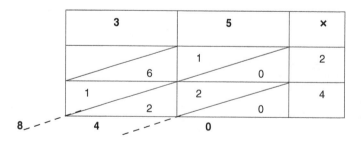

The digits at the top of the grid are multiplied in turn by those down the side. The answers to each of these multiplications are written in the boxes, the tens value being written above the diagonal line and the units value below. Finally, the numbers in each diagonal are added, carrying as necessary to the next diagonal.

This method can also be applied to the multiplication of decimals.

For more information on Gelosia multiplication, see the section on multiplication of decimals in Chapter 3.

REFLECTIVE TASK

In the above example, the Gelosia multiplication method is used to calculate 35 × 24. Before reading on, take some time now to study the grid and explain (using a clear understanding of place value) how it works.

How does the Gelosia method work?
In the above example, 35 × 24 is worked out. This is the same as multiplying (30 + 5) by (20 + 4). Let's take the 5 × 20 part of this equation. Can you see what is entered into the sections of the grid when 5 × 2 is calculated? Yes, 10 has been entered into those sections, but the 10 really represents 100 (5 × 20). The 1 sits in the hundreds 'column' and the 0 in the tens. So, when all the digits in each of the diagonal 'columns' are added together, the correct total is found. The diagram below might be helpful to provide further explanation:

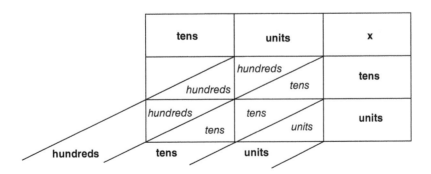

PRACTICAL TASK

Learn your times tables! All of the above strategies for multiplication become more efficient with rapid recall of table facts. All children in primary schools need to be fluent in their recall of table facts so if you do not already know your times tables to 12, it is important that you learn and become confident with them.

The following Research Summary outlines the importance of quick recall of number facts:

RESEARCH SUMMARY

Askew and William (1995) present evidence to indicate that children who are able to recall number facts, but are also able to use their deduction skills to work out things they cannot recall, make more progress than those who have access to only one approach. This is because each approach supports the other. The authors also consider the issue of children relying too heavily on counting to solve arithmetical problems, rather than developing a knowledge of number facts. Despite being able to use counting techniques to produce correct answers, this over-dependence removes the need to learn number facts, which in turn restricts children's ability to develop deductive approaches.

Both of these issues are also discussed by Gray (2008, page 87) who states that the child who has progressed from relying on counting techniques to knowing facts possesses a powerful tool with which to achieve success in arithmetic and goes on to say that those who know facts and use them flexibly find arithmetic far easier than those who have to carry out counting procedures.

Division

As above with the other operations, there is a wide range of strategies that can be used to divide numbers. This section will start by considering informal written methods, which are frequently derived from mental methods. It will also outline some more standard methods of dividing using pencil and paper calculations.

Repeated subtraction

One of the earliest methods of dividing involves knowledge of the relationship between subtraction and division. Once it is realised that division can be seen as repeated subtraction, then this fact can be used to solve simple division problems. For example, $24 \div 6$:

This can be calculated as $24 - 6 = 18$

$18 - 6 = 12$

$12 - 6 = 6$

$6 - 6 = 0$ How many times has 6 been subtracted? 4

It can quickly be seen that this method is rather limited and would be very cumbersome for large calculations. However, knowledge of multiplication by 10, 100, 1000, etc. can be used along with repeated subtraction to extend this method. For example, $28875 \div 231$:

$$231 \times 100 = 23100 \qquad \begin{array}{r} 28875 \\ -23100 \\ \hline 5775 \end{array}$$

$$231 \times 10 = 2310 \qquad \begin{array}{r} 5775 \\ -2310 \\ \hline 3465 \end{array}$$

$$231 \times 10 = 2310 \qquad \begin{array}{r} 3465 \\ -2310 \\ \hline 1155 \end{array}$$

$1155 - 231 = 924$ How many times has 231 been subtracted

$924 - 231 = 693$ from 28875? Simply add to find out:

$693 - 231 = 462$ $100 + 10 + 10 + 1 + 1 + 1 + 1 + 1 = 125$

$462 - 231 = 231$

$231 - 231 = 0$

Traditional long division

The traditional method for long division, frequently taught as a standard algorithm, is really a shorthand version of a method not unlike the repeated subtraction method shown above. The traditional algorithm for 7404 ÷ 6 is as follows:

```
    1 2 3 4
6 | 74 0 4
    6            (6×1, hence 1 in the thousands column of the answer)
   ──
   14
   12            (6×2, hence 2 in the hundreds column of the answer)
   ──
    20
    18           (6×3, hence 3 in the tens column of the answer)
   ──
    24
    24           (6×4, hence 4 in the units column of the answer)
    ──
     0
```

This should really be viewed as shorthand for the following arrangement if this method is to have any meaning:

```
   1234
6 | 7404
   6000         (6×1000)
   ────
   1404
   1200         (6×200)
   ────
    204
    180         (6×30)
    ───
     24
     24         (6×4)
    ───
      0
```

Traditional long division (abbreviated)

It is possible to attempt the above question using an abbreviated form of long division. Some people are taught this as their standard algorithm. This method is illustrated using the same example, 7404 ÷ 6.

```
    1  2  3  4       Here, 6 is divided into each of the digits in turn;
6 | 7¹4²0²4         any remainder is 'carried over' to the next column.
```

There are certain fundamental laws which underpin all work in arithmetic. It is important that you have a very clear understanding of these in order to support children's mathematical development.

Precedence – BODMAS

Before considering the laws governing the operations, it is important to understand that precedence is given to particular operations when working out a complex expression. For example, how would you solve:

$$8 - 3 \times (4 + 2) + 16 \div 4 - 2 \times 3$$

If the expression is attempted simply working left to right, the answer obtained would be:

$$8 - 3 = 5, \text{ then} \times 6 \text{ (i.e. } 4 + 2) = 30, \text{ next} + 16 = 46,$$

$$\text{now} \div 4 = 11.5, \text{ then} - 2 = 9.5, \text{ finally} \times 3 = 28.5$$

This is incorrect, however, due to mathematical convention which gives a specific order for tackling such problems. The order can be summarised as BODMAS. BODMAS stands for:

B – brackets

O – of

D – division

M – multiplication

A – addition

S – subtraction

When solving expressions such as the one above, convention dictates that the brackets are solved first, followed by any 'of', division and multiplication operations, finally addition and subtraction are considered. For the above example this gives:

$$
\begin{aligned}
8 - 3 \times (4 + 2) &+ 16 \div 4 - 2 \times 3 \\
= 8 - 3 \times 6 &+ 16 \div 4 - 2 \times 3 \qquad \text{(tackling brackets first)} \\
= 8 - 18 &+ 4 - 6 \qquad \text{(now working out the} \times \text{and} \div) \\
= -12 & \qquad \text{(finally completing the} + \text{and} -)
\end{aligned}
$$

Precedence is referred to differently in some countries. This is explored further in *Primary Mathematics: Extending Knowledge in Practice* (Learning Matters, 2008).

PRACTICAL TASK

Try the following example before looking at the workings shown:

$$3 + 4 \times (3 - 1) + 6 \div 3 - 5$$

Applying the BODMAS order of precedence gives:

$$3 + 4 \times (3 - 1) + 6 \div 3 - 5$$
$$= 3 + 4 \times 2 \quad\quad + 6 \div 3 - 5 \quad\quad \text{(brackets first)}$$
$$= 3 + \quad 8 \quad\quad + \quad 2 \; - 5 \quad\quad (\text{now} \times \text{and} \div)$$
$$= 8 \quad\quad\quad\quad\quad\quad\quad\quad\quad (\text{finally} + \text{and} -)$$

The laws of arithmetic

Having considered the order of precedence of the operations, it is necessary to understand the structural laws which apply. There are three laws of arithmetic that underpin calculations using the four operations. These laws are:

- the commutative law;
- the associative law;
- the distributive law.

The commutative law

This law basically states that the order in which the operation is performed makes no difference to the answer. For which of the four operations (addition, subtraction, multiplication and division) does this hold true? Using some numerical examples it can be seen that:

$$6 + 3 = 3 + 6 \quad \text{but} \quad 6 - 3 \neq 3 - 6$$
$$6 \times 3 = 3 \times 6 \quad \text{but} \quad 6 \div 3 \neq 3 \div 6$$

Generally, the operations of addition and multiplication are commutative for any numbers a and b. Subtraction and division are not commutative.

$$a + b = b + a \qquad a \times b = b \times a$$
$$a - b \neq b - a \qquad a \div b \neq b \div a$$

The associative law

This law means that numbers can be regrouped to simplify a question while making no difference to the answer. The fact that numbers can be grouped and combined in different ways is very helpful during certain calculations where a reordering of the component numbers will ease the difficulty of the calculation. This is essential for the development of appropriate mental calculation strategies. For which of the four rules does this hold true? Using some numerical examples it can be seen that:

$$(2 + 3) + 7 = 2 + (3 + 7) \quad \text{but} \quad (10 - 2) - 1 \neq 10 - (2 - 1)$$
$$(2 \times 3) \times 7 = 2 \times (3 \times 7) \quad \text{but} \quad (12 \div 6) \div 2 \neq 12 \div (6 \div 2)$$

Generally, the operations of addition and multiplication are associative for any numbers a, b and c. Subtraction and division are not associative.

$$(a + b) + c = a + (b + c) \qquad (a \times b) \times c = a \times (b \times c)$$
$$(a - b) - c \neq a - (b - c) \qquad (a \times b) \div c \neq a \div (b \div c)$$

The distributive law

The distributive law is so called as it involves one operation being 'distributed out' over another operation. A simple example of this law is to answer the following problem mentally. You go into a shop and buy five pairs of socks costing £4.99 a pair. How much do you spend?

The obvious way to answer this is to say, 'That's 5 × £5 take away 5p which gives £24.95.' How can this be written down?

$$5 \times (£5 - 1p) = (5 \times £5) - (5 \times 1p)$$

Because £4.99 = £5 − 1p

Generally, this distributive law of multiplication over subtraction can be written:

$$a \times (b - c) = (a \times b) - (a \times c)$$

This also holds true for multiplication over addition:

$$a \times (b + c) = (a \times b) + (a \times c)$$

But does it hold true for division over addition and subtraction? This is a very interesting question. Consider the following example for multiplication over addition:

$$2 \times (3 + 4) = (2 \times 3) + (2 \times 4)$$

Due to the commutative law, this would give exactly the same answer if it was written:

$$2 \div (4 + 6) \neq (2 \div 4) + (2 \div 6)$$

Next, consider the following numerical example for division over addition:

$$2 \div (4 + 6) \neq (2 \times 4) + (2 \div 6)$$

However,

$$(4 + 6) \div 2 = (4 \div 2) + (6 \div 2)$$

Because of this, division is said to be *right* distributive over addition and subtraction. This means that as long as the **dividend** (number being divided) is the number that is 'split' the law holds. However, if it is the **divisor** (the number dividing into the dividend) which is split, then the law does not hold. Put more crudely, the division needs to be on the right side of the brackets, hence right distributive.

Expressed generally : $a \div (b + c) \neq (a \div b) + (a \div c)$
however : $(a + b) \div c = (a \div c) + (b \div c)$
and also : $(a - b) \div c = (a \div c) - (b \div c)$

Negative numbers

Integers are positive or negative whole numbers. When considering the four rules of number it is important to consider how they relate to calculations involving negative numbers. Take as an example the equations $4 - 3 = 1$ and $3 - (-4) = 7$.

- 4 – 3 can be read as 'find the difference between 4 and 3' with the answer being 1.

- Similarly 3 – (–4) can be read as 'find the difference between 3 and –4'. Looking at the number line it is easy to see that there is a difference of seven. This is much more convincing than just remembering that 'two minuses make a plus', thus making 3 – (–4) into 3 + 4 without any understanding.

Calculations with negative numbers can be simplified with the use of a number line:

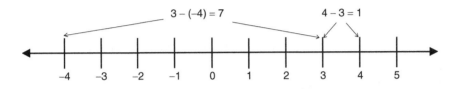

- When adding a negative number, the commutative property of addition can be used. This means that $2 + (–1) = (–1) + 2$ and $(–1) + 2 = 1$.

Multiplication and division of negative numbers also gives rise to certain rules, but how are these rules arrived at?

Above it has been shown how 'two minuses make a plus' but how does this relate to multiplication?

- Consider the problem $6 \times (–6)$. It is clear that this is 6 lots of –6, which is equal to –36. But what about $(–6) \times (–6)$? This will give the negative, or opposite, of $6 \times (–6)$, so if $6 \times (–6) = –36$ then $(–6) \times (–6)$ must be equal to 36.

- This is also true for division. Consider $(–36) \div (–6)$. This is one way of writing how many –6s in –36. The answer to this is clearly 6. Therefore when considering $36 \div (–6)$ the answer is the negative, or opposite, of the previous answer i.e. –6.

A SUMMARY OF KEY POINTS

- Our decimal place value system uses only ten digits. The position of a digit relative to any other digits in the number determines its value. The larger groupings are always on the left. Numbers are read from left to right.

(Continued)

(Continued)

- The four number operations are related to each other in specific ways. Addition is the inverse of subtraction and vice versa. Multiplication and division are the inverse of each other. Multiplication can be seen as repeated addition and division as repeated subtraction.
- Prior to attempting to solve any complex expressions, it is necessary to know the order of precedence of the operations. This order can be summarised as BODMAS.
- There are certain structural laws underpinning arithmetic. Addition and multiplication are both commutative and associative. Multiplication is distributive over addition and subtraction. Division is right distributive over addition and subtraction.
- There is a need for effective mental calculation strategies to underpin all written work.

M-LEVEL EXTENSION

Look again at the Research Summaries in this chapter. Reflect on the findings. Then go to Ofsted's website (www.ofsted.gov.uk) and download a copy of *Mathematics: Understanding the Score - Improving Practice in Mathematics Teaching at Primary Level* (Ofsted, 2007). Consider the exemplar material on number and compare the approaches described with practice that you have observed in schools. What implications are there for your own knowledge and understanding and in turn for your teaching to develop children's understanding of number?

FURTHER READING

Cook, H. (2007) *Mathematics for Primary and Early Years: Developing Subject Knowledge,* 2nd edn. London: Sage. This book gives even coverage to the National Curriculum subjects. It has a useful introduction that considers why people may have concerns about learning mathematics and how you may overcome these through thinking about what kind of learner you are.

DfE (2011) *Teachers' Standards*. Available at https://www.gov.uk/government/uploads/system/uploads/attachment_data/file/301107/Teachers__Standards.pdf

Hansen, A. (2008) *Primary Mathematics: Extending Knowledge in Practice*. Exeter: Learning Matters. This book offers classroom-based case studies that consider some of the most difficult areas of the primary mathematics curriculum to teach. As well as considering pedagogical issues, it also discusses the subject knowledge required by the teacher to teach the curriculum effectively.

Haylock, D. (2014) *Mathematics Explained for Primary Teachers*, 5th edn. London: Sage. As the title suggests, this book explains much of the content of the primary mathematics curriculum. It also addresses key teaching points and gives opportunities to try some self-assessment questions in each area, to further support your subject knowledge development.

Suggate, J., Davis, A. and Goulding, M. (2017) *Mathematical Knowledge for Primary Teachers*, 5th edn. London: Routledge. This book offers another source for developing your subject knowledge. Its chatty style and comprehensive coverage is helpful. Over half of the book is dedicated to number.

Thompson, I. (ed.) (2010) *Issues in Teaching Numeracy in Primary Schools*, 2nd edn. Buckingham: Open University Press. This book addresses many issues of current debate within the development of numeracy in schools. It tackles the direct classroom-based issues as well as considering children as learners and how to develop appropriate visual images to support the development of numeracy.

3

Number: fractions, decimals and percentages

Teachers' Standards

A teacher must:

3.   Demonstrate good subject and curriculum knowledge

- have a secure knowledge of the relevant subject(s) and curriculum areas, foster and maintain pupils' interest in the subject, and address misunderstandings
- demonstrate a critical understanding of developments in the subject and curriculum areas, and promote the value of scholarship

4.   Plan and teach well structured lessons

- impart knowledge and develop understanding through effective use of lesson time
- promote a love of learning and children's intellectual curiosity
- contribute to the design and provision of an engaging curriculum within the relevant subject area(s)

8.   Fulfil wider professional responsibilities

- take responsibility for improving teaching through appropriate professional development

Curriculum context

Early Years Foundation Stage

The Early Years Foundation Stage recognises the importance of certain key skills in mathematical development. These include counting and working with numbers. The mathematical understanding of the children should be developed through games, songs, stories and play to encourage experimenting with numbers, including those larger than 10.

National Curriculum programmes of study

Within the Mathematics National Curriculum, the Number Programme of Study states the knowledge, skills and understanding which are to be taught throughout Key Stages 1 and 2.

At Key Stage 1, the principal focus of mathematics teaching is to ensure that children develop confidence and mental fluency with numbers. This involves an initial understanding of fractions. Children need to recognise, name and write simple fractions (such as $\frac{1}{2}$; $\frac{1}{4}$; $\frac{3}{4}$).

During Lower Key Stage 2, children are expected to expand their understanding of fractions considerably. They learn to recognise, find and write fractions of a discrete set of objects. They must also recognise and be able to show equivalent fractions with small denominators, and add and subtract fractions with the same denominator within one whole. Beyond this, they need to be able to solve problems that involve all of these.

In Upper Key Stage 2, children's understanding is expanded to include decimals and percentages. Children are expected to (for example): read and write decimal numbers as fractions; solve problems involving numbers up to three decimal places and understand that per cent relates to 'number of parts per 100'. They must also be able to solve problems which require knowing percentage and decimal equivalents of some fractions.

Number: fractions, decimals and percentages

Introduction

This chapter continues on from the last in exploring the structural laws underpinning arithmetic. The focus here is fractions, decimals and percentages. The chapter also discusses the concepts of forming equalities and inequalities, identifying rational and irrational numbers, and representing numbers in standard form and using index form.

Fractions

REFLECTIVE TASK

Lotti is asked to add the following fractions: $\frac{1}{4} + \frac{1}{2} + \frac{1}{2}$

She tackles the problem as follows:

$$\frac{1}{4} + \frac{1}{2} + \frac{1}{2} = \frac{1}{4} + \frac{2}{4} = \frac{3}{8}$$

What does this tell you about her understanding of fractions and addition of fractions?

It is clear that Lotti does not understand that the denominator indicates the number of fractional parts the unit has been divided into, while the numerator indicates how many parts of this size there are. An understanding of this is essential if she is to successfully add fractions either mentally or using a pencil and paper method.

$$\frac{1 \leftarrow \text{numerator}}{2 \leftarrow \text{denominator}}$$

Fractions have formed a useful part of mathematics since ancient Egyptian times. Because they did not a have a place value system, the Egyptians only used unit fractions (e.g. $\frac{1}{2}, \frac{1}{3}, \frac{1}{9}, \frac{1}{24}$ etc.) as to attempt anything more complex would have involved extremely cumbersome calculations. Think of the Babylonian system which used base 60. When considering unit fractions, base 60 is very useful, because 60 has so many factors. For example, $\frac{1}{2}, \frac{1}{3}, \frac{1}{4}, \frac{1}{5}, \frac{1}{6}, \frac{1}{10}, \frac{1}{12}, \frac{1}{15}, \frac{1}{20}, \frac{1}{30}$ would all give whole number answers as fractions of an hour. It is important to remember what the notation means: $\frac{1}{2}$ is a form of writing 1 unit divided into 2 parts. Similarly $\frac{3}{5}$ can be read as 5 divided into 3 groups.

RESEARCH SUMMARY

Why do children struggle with fractions?

Kieren (1976) was one of the first authors to point out that fractions are not a single concept for children to understand, but instead comprise five different components or interpretations.

1. The first of these is the 'part–whole' component, whereby a whole object is divided into equal parts and some are selected. This is the way that most children first encounter fractions, for example in relation to three-quarters of a cake.

2. The second is the '**quotient**' component, which relates to the division of whole number quantities to produce fractions, for example when 3 pizzas are shared equally between 4 people to produce the answer 3/4.

3. The third is the '**ratio**' component, in which fractions are used to compare the relative sizes of two objects, for example where one length of ribbon is three-quarters of the length of another.

4. The 'measure' component is usually associated with the marking of fractions on number lines, thus providing a possible way of considering the addition and subtraction of fractions.

5. The 'operator' component utilises fractions in a multiplicative sense, for example by calculating three-quarters of 15 objects.

It is the multi-faceted nature of fractions that makes it a difficult concept for children to understand and it is therefore vitally important that teachers employ an appropriate range of contexts, structures, models and images.

3 Number: fractions, decimals and percentages

The use of fractions falls into two main areas:

- as a *measurement* such as $\frac{1}{4}$ hour or $\frac{1}{2}$ kilometre, where the fraction is being used to express part of a unit (in this case hours and kilometres);
- as an *operator* on another number, as in $\frac{1}{4}$ of 24.

Within these areas there are five different ways of considering fractions. These are listed below, with examples for one quarter and four fifths:

- Part of a complete unit or 'whole':

- A comparison between a subset and a whole set:

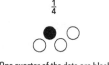   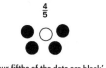

- A number, the point on a line between two whole numbers:

- The result of division of whole numbers:

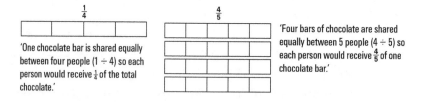

- Comparing the sizes of two measurements or two sets of objects:

46

For more information on comparing sizes, see the section on ratio and proportion, later in this chapter.

Equivalent fractions

One of the most important concepts in the development of the understanding of
fractions is that of **equivalence**. Equivalent fractions have the same value and
so appear on a number line in the same place.

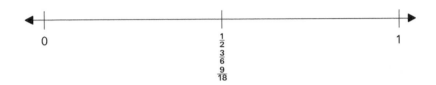

A useful prompt to help see these 'fraction families' is the fraction wall. The
recognition of the numerical pattern of these fractions is also vital. For example:

(a) $\dfrac{1}{2}, \dfrac{2}{4}, \dfrac{4}{8}, \dfrac{8}{16}$ (b) $\dfrac{1}{2}, \dfrac{2}{4}, \dfrac{3}{6}, \dfrac{4}{8}$

What would the next equivalent fraction be in each case?

(a) the numerator and the denominator are both being multiplied by 2 to ensure
the fractions are equivalent to $\frac{1}{2}$, hence the next fraction in the family would
be $\frac{16}{32}$

(b) the numerator is increasing by 1 each time, the denominator is double the
numerator as these fractions are all equivalent to $\frac{1}{2}$. Hence, the next fraction
in the family would be $\frac{5}{10}$

One whole															
One half								One half							
One quarter				One quarter				One quarter				One quarter			
$\frac{1}{8}$		$\frac{1}{8}$		$\frac{1}{8}$		$\frac{1}{8}$		$\frac{1}{8}$		$\frac{1}{8}$		$\frac{1}{8}$		$\frac{1}{8}$	
$\frac{1}{16}$	$\frac{1}{16}$	$\frac{1}{16}$	$\frac{1}{16}$	$\frac{1}{16}$	$\frac{1}{16}$	$\frac{1}{16}$	$\frac{1}{16}$	$\frac{1}{16}$	$\frac{1}{16}$	$\frac{1}{16}$	$\frac{1}{16}$	$\frac{1}{16}$	$\frac{1}{16}$	$\frac{1}{16}$	$\frac{1}{16}$

3 Number: fractions, decimals and percentages

Using the wall it is easy to see that $\frac{1}{2}=\frac{2}{4}=\frac{4}{8}$ and that $\frac{3}{4}=\frac{6}{8}$ and $\frac{1}{4}=\frac{2}{8}$ and so on.

One whole											
One third				One third				One third			
One sixth		One sixth		One sixth		One sixth		One sixth		One sixth	
$\frac{1}{9}$		$\frac{1}{9}$		$\frac{1}{9}$		$\frac{1}{9}$		$\frac{1}{9}$		$\frac{1}{9}$	
$\frac{1}{12}$	$\frac{1}{12}$	$\frac{1}{12}$	$\frac{1}{12}$	$\frac{1}{12}$	$\frac{1}{12}$	$\frac{1}{12}$	$\frac{1}{12}$	$\frac{1}{12}$	$\frac{1}{12}$	$\frac{1}{12}$	$\frac{1}{12}$

Using this wall it can be seen that $\frac{1}{3} = \frac{2}{6} = \frac{4}{12}$ and $\frac{1}{3} = \frac{3}{9}$ and so on.

Numerically, for any fraction, an equivalent fraction can be found by multiplying the numerator and denominator by the same number. For example:

$\frac{4}{7}$ is equivalent to $\frac{16}{28}$ (the numerator and denominator have been multiplied by 4

The same applies when dividing the numerator and denominator by the same number. For example:

$\frac{36}{63}$ is equivalent to $\frac{4}{7}$ (the numerator and denominator have been divided by 9)

Finding equivalent fractions is closely linked to 'cancelling' fractions during calculations. If the numerator and denominator are 'cancelled' in order to simplify the fraction, then the new fraction will be equivalent to the original one. For example:

$\frac{6}{18}$ can be simplified to $\frac{1}{3}$ (by dividing numerator and denominator by 6)

$\frac{6}{18}$ and $\frac{1}{3}$ are equivalent fractions so would appear on a number line in the same place.

Sometimes it is easier to cancel in two or more stages:

$\frac{96}{132}$	(divide numerator and denominator by 3)	$\frac{32}{44}$	(divide numerator and denominator by 4)	$\frac{8}{11}$

Comparing fractions

Comparing fractions is quite straightforward if the denominators are the same (referred to as having a **common denominator**), e.g. $\frac{5}{7}$ is bigger than $\frac{3}{7}$. This is clear, as the denominator, in this case 7, indicates the number of fractional parts the unit has been divided into (sevenths here), whilst the numerator indicates the number of parts (here 5 and 3, and 5 is greater than 3). This is harder to see if the fractions have different denominators.

Is $\frac{3}{4}$ bigger than $\frac{5}{7}$? Here the denominators are 4 and 7. In order to compare them, the fractions need to be expressed in terms of units which have been divided into the same number of fractional parts, i.e. they need to have a common denominator. The lowest number which is a multiple of both 4 and 7 is 28.

$\frac{3}{4}$ is equivalent to $\frac{21}{28}$ (top and bottom multiplied by 7)

$\frac{5}{7}$ is equivalent to $\frac{20}{28}$ (top and bottom multiplied by 4)

From this it is clear that $\frac{3}{4}$ is larger than $\frac{5}{7}$.

Finding equivalent fractions, cancelling and comparing are all necessary skills when calculating using fractions.

Addition of fractions

When adding fractions it is important to remember that the denominators are not added. This is quite obvious really when considering what the denominators actually represent. The denominator represents the number of parts the unit has been divided into. Taking an example, adding two fractions with a common denominator gives:

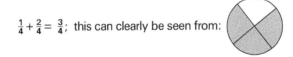

$\frac{1}{4} + \frac{2}{4} = \frac{3}{4}$; this can clearly be seen from:

If the fractions to be added do not have a common denominator, then equivalent fractions need to be found which do have a common denominator to allow the addition to take place. For example:

$$\frac{1}{5} + \frac{3}{4}$$

The lowest common denominator is the lowest number which is a multiple of both 5 and 4, i.e. the lowest common multiple, in this case 20.

Next, work out the equivalent fractions expressed in twentieths:

$\frac{1}{5}$ – in order to achieve twentieths the denominator was multiplied by 4. To keep the fraction equivalent, the numerator must also be multiplied by 4, giving:

$$\frac{1}{5} = \frac{4}{20}$$

$\frac{3}{4}$ – in order to achieve twentieths the denominator was multiplied by 5. Again, to ensure equivalence, the numerator must be multiplied by the same, giving:

$$\frac{3}{4} = \frac{15}{20}$$

Rewriting the addition using equivalent fractions expressed in twentieths gives:

$$\frac{4}{20} + \frac{15}{20} + \frac{19}{20}$$

Subtraction of fractions

The process of subtracting fractions is very similar to adding them. If the denominators are the same it is very straightforward. If they do not have a common denominator, as with addition, one needs to be found in order to identify equivalent fractions to subtract. For example:

$$\frac{3}{4} - \frac{1}{6}$$

The lowest common denominator (or lowest common multiple) here is 12.

Expressing $\frac{3}{4}$ in twelfths gives $\frac{9}{12}$

Expressing $\frac{1}{6}$ in twelfths gives $\frac{2}{12}$

Substituting these equivalent fractions into the subtraction problem gives:

$$\frac{9}{12} - \frac{2}{12} - \frac{7}{12}$$

Multiplication of fractions

In order to multiply fractions it is necessary to consider what is happening when you multiply any numbers. What does 2×5 actually mean? The meaning can be stated in a range of ways including 'twice 5' or 'twice as much as 5'. Consider what the meaning would be if a fractional value was substituted, e.g. $2 \times \frac{1}{4}$. This could be said to mean 'twice as much as $\frac{1}{4}$'. Therefore $\frac{1}{2} \times \frac{1}{4}$ can be read as '$\frac{1}{2}$ as much as $\frac{1}{4}$' or '$\frac{1}{2}$ of $\frac{1}{4}$'. One quarter can be shown as:

$\frac{1}{4}$ of the unit

Next, find one half of one quarter of the unit:

Here $\frac{1}{2}$ of $\frac{1}{4}$ of the unit has been revealed

This illustrates that $\frac{1}{2} \times \frac{1}{4} = \frac{1}{8}$

Generally, it can be seen that in order to multiply the two fractions the numerators were multiplied together and the denominators were multiplied together. This can be expressed as:

$$\frac{a}{b} \times \frac{c}{d} = \frac{a \times c}{b \times d} \text{ for any numbers a, b, c, d}$$

Division of fractions

In order to fully explain division of fractions, it is necessary to find a context which structures the problem clearly – one such context is food. Consider the problem $\frac{1}{2} \div 4$. This could also be written as $\frac{1}{2} \div \frac{4}{1}$.

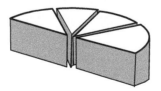

Half a cake needs to be shared between 4 people. How much cake will each person get? Each person will get $\frac{1}{4}$ of the $\frac{1}{2}$ cake that is left, i.e. $\frac{1}{8}$ of the cake.

From this it can be seen that an equivalent way of writing $\frac{1}{2} \div \frac{4}{1}$ is as $\frac{1}{4}$ of $\frac{1}{2}$ or $\frac{1}{4} \times \frac{1}{2}$. Because multiplication is commutative, $\frac{1}{4} \times \frac{1}{2}$ can be rewritten as $\frac{1}{2} \times \frac{1}{4}$

Another example: $\frac{3}{4} \div \frac{2}{3}$

This is the same as $\frac{3}{2}$ of $\frac{3}{4}$ or $\frac{3}{4} \times \frac{3}{2}$. So

$$\frac{3}{4} \div \frac{2}{3} = \frac{3}{4} \times \frac{3}{2} = \frac{9}{8} = 1\frac{1}{8}$$

Decimals

The decimal system was popularised by John Napier (1550–1617). He was a Scottish landowner for whom mathematics was his chief hobby. He was particularly interested in trigonometry and computation. In 1614 he published the first book of logarithmic tables which had taken him 20 years to complete. He also invented 'Napier's bones', a calculating system using numbered rods.

Decimal fractions are an extension of place value and are not a new set of numbers. The decimal representation of a number is actually based on the fractions $\frac{1}{10}, \frac{1}{100}, \frac{1}{1000}$ etc. This should be remembered when **ordering** decimals. 0.35 and 0.09 are $\frac{35}{100}$ (35 hundredths) and $\frac{9}{100}$ (9 hundredths) respectively.

Decimal notation is used and seen with calculators, computers, money, petrol pumps and measurements, so it would seem increasingly likely that the use of fractions will become more common during conversation and certain specific occasions rather than in mathematical computation.

'I am going to cut this cake into quarters,' is easier to say than, 'I'm going to cut this cake into 0.25s.' Conversely 0.25 + 0.5 + 0.2 is an easier calculation than $\frac{1}{4} + \frac{1}{2} + \frac{1}{5}$

Addition and subtraction of decimal numbers are exactly the same as with whole numbers. When multiplying and dividing by powers of 10 it is important to remember that the decimal point is fixed and that 0 is used as a place holder. It is possible to see from the figure below that when multiplying by ten the digits move one place to the left and when dividing by ten they move one place to the right.

	Th	H	T	U	.	$\frac{1}{10}$	$\frac{1}{100}$	$\frac{1}{1000}$
1.1 × 1000	1	1	0	0				
1.1 × 100		1	1	0				
1.1 × 10			1	1				
1.1 × 1				1	.	1		
1.1 ÷ 10				0	.	1	1	
1.1 ÷ 100				0	.	0	1	1

(Notice that the whole numbers do not require a decimal point.)

When multiplying and dividing by decimal numbers, remember that decimals are a representation of fractions so $0.1 = \frac{1}{10}$. Knowing this, work through the following calculations:

$$500 \times 0.1 = 500 \times \frac{1}{10} = 500 \div 10 = \frac{(500)}{10} = 50$$

$$500 \div 0.1 = 500 \div \frac{1}{10} = 500 \times 10 = 5000$$

It may be helpful to 'read' the calculations using multiplication of whole numbers as a 'model'. For example, 5 × 2 can be interpreted as 2 groups of 5 or 5 groups of 2 (because of the commutative nature of multiplication) and the answer is 10. Similarly 500 × 0.1 can be seen as 500 groups of 0.1, which is 50.

10 ÷ 2 can be read as 'how many 2s in 10?' and so 500 ÷ 0.1 is 'how many 0.1s in 500?' with the answer being 5000.

It is important to have a realistic idea of the estimated answer when working with decimals. For example, the answer to 4.67 × 3.23 will be between 12 and 20 because 4 × 3 = 12 (taking the whole numbers below the decimal numbers stated) and 5 × 4 = 20 (taking the whole numbers above the decimal numbers stated). It is also possible to say it is approximately equal to 5 × 3, by rounding to the nearest whole numbers. This is particularly useful in calculations where estimation can be used to check if the answer looks to be within a sensible range.

Division solely involving whole numbers results in an answer which is smaller than the dividend. The dividend is the number that is to be divided; the divisor is the number by which the dividend is divided. For example:

$$\text{dividend} \rightarrow \frac{24}{6} = 4 \leftarrow \text{quotient}$$
$$\text{divisor} \rightarrow$$

When dividing two decimal numbers less than 1, the answer is a larger number. The number line can be used to illustrate examples of division and multiplication involving decimals. This is because both multiplication and division are based on repeated addition and subtraction.

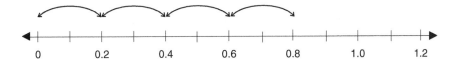

This number line illustrates 0.2 × 4 = 0.8 or 0.8 ÷ 0.2 = 4

Addition and subtraction of decimals

Because the decimal system was devised to show fractional parts within one number, through the use of the decimal point, it is straightforward to add or subtract decimals.

Addition and subtraction are virtually the same as with whole numbers – do remember that if setting out a calculation vertically, it is vital to ensure the decimal points 'line up' to keep the place value set throughout the problem.

For example, adding 25.46 and 7.523 gives:

$$\begin{array}{r} 25.46 \\ +\ \ 7.523 \\ \hline 32.983 \\ {\scriptstyle 1} \end{array}$$

Where attempting subtraction involving decomposition, it is important to remember that 0 is used as a place holder. For example, 25.46 – 7.523:

$$\begin{array}{r} {\scriptstyle 1\,1\,4\ \ 1\,5\,1} \\ 2\cancel{5}.\cancel{4}\cancel{6}\cancel{0} \\ -7.523 \\ \hline 17.937 \end{array}$$ 0 inserted as a place holder to aid the calculation

Multiplication of decimals

Formal multiplication of decimals can be undertaken in a number of ways. Some of these methods structure the place value concept, others do not. One method, which was quite widely taught as a formal algorithm, involved completely ignoring the place value structure. This can be seen in the following working for 6.4 × 2.3:

$$\begin{array}{r} 6.4 \\ \times\ 2.3 \\ \hline 19{,}2 \\ 1280 \\ \hline 14.72 \\ {\scriptstyle 1} \end{array}$$

19,2 ←——— Decimal point is ignored here

14.72——→ The number of digits in total after the decimal points in the question is found and the decimal point is reinserted to allow this number of decimal places in the answer

This method obviously does nothing to develop a place value understanding for decimals. It is possible to use the standard long multiplication algorithm with decimals and structure it to keep the place value accurately determined. The same question might be attempted as follows:

6.4

×2.3

$\overline{1.9_12} \rightarrow 0.3 \times 6.4$

$12.8 \rightarrow 2 \times 6.4$

$\overline{14_1.72}$

To remind yourself how Gelosia multiplication works, look back to Chapter 2.

As mentioned in Chapter 2, it is possible to use the Gelosia method of multiplication when multiplying decimals. This method has place value built into the structure and can be infinitely extended either side of the decimal point.

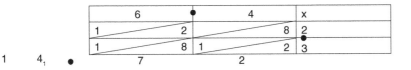

In this case, to position the decimal point correctly in the answer, imagine lines extending from the decimal points in the question, one line vertical, the other horizontal. These lines meet at a diagonal. It is at the end of this diagonal that the decimal point should be placed. As can be seen in the example above, this works since extended lines from the decimal points in the questions will always meet at the diagonal separating units from tenths – place value is built into the structure.

Division of decimals

Division of decimals is very straightforward providing you can divide whole numbers. If the dividend (number to be divided) is a decimal number and the divisor (number dividing into the dividend) is a whole number, the calculation is carried out in exactly the same way as for standard long division. For example, $773.112 \div 24$, using the abbreviated algorithm:

$$32.213$$
$$24\overline{)77^53.^51^31^72}$$

In order to undertake decimal division involving a divisor that is a decimal number in the most straightforward way, it is necessary to undertake an equivalent calculation. The first thing to do is to multiply the divisor by a power of 10 in order to transform it into a whole number. Having done that, the dividend must be multiplied by the same power of 10 in order that the quotient will remain unchanged. For example, in order to divide 0.2 by 0.5, the divisor (in this case 0.5) needs to be changed into a whole number. To do this it must be multiplied by 10, giving 5. Having multiplied the divisor by 10 it is necessary to multiply the dividend by 10, giving 2. Why does this work? This can be shown very simply using algebra:

x divided by y is the same as 10x divided by 10y because

$$\frac{10x}{10y} = \frac{x}{y}$$

Try using this to solve 0.448 ÷ 0.14:

First multiply the divisor (0.14) by 100 to make it a whole number, i.e. 14. Next multiply the dividend by the same number to ensure the quotient remains unchanged, giving 0.448 × 100 = 44.8. Now divide using an appropriate algorithm:

$$14\overline{\smash)44.^28}\ \ ^{3.2}$$

To find out more on interpreting decimals on a calculator, see Chapter 7, *Primary Mathematics: Teaching Theory and Practice* (Learning Matters, 2018).

Converting fractions and decimals

In order to convert a fraction to a decimal the fraction is simply treated as the division that it represents, e.g.:

To convert $\frac{3}{4}$ into a decimal, 3 is divided by 4, thus $4\overline{\smash)3.^30^20}\ \ ^{0.75}$

Converting back from a decimal to a fraction involves identifying the fractional parts represented by the decimal, e.g.:

0.75 could also be read as 7 tenths and 5 hundredths or as 75 hundredths. It is this second version, 75 hundredths, where the decimal is expressed in terms of just one fractional part, that enables the fractional equivalence to be shown:

$0.75 = \dfrac{75}{100}$ which can be simplified by dividing top and bottom by 25 giving $\dfrac{3}{4}$

Try to convert 0.125 into a fraction before looking at the workings below.

0.125 represents 125 thousandths or $\dfrac{125}{1000}$. This can be simplified by dividing by 125 to give $\dfrac{1}{8}$

Using mental strategies to calculate with fractions and decimals

Knowing some fraction and decimal relationships by heart is useful to enable a flexible approach to calculation.

> **PRACTICAL TASK**
>
> What is 0.125 × 160? Can you calculate the answer mentally?
>
> In order to calculate the answer efficiently and accurately, knowing that 0.125 equals $\frac{1}{8}$ is useful. Undertaking the following steps it is possible to calculate the answer mentally:
>
> 1. Start with 160: 160
> 2. Halve 160: 80 (to find $\frac{1}{2}$)
> 3. Halve 80: 40 (to find $\frac{1}{4}$)
> 4. Halve 40: 20 (to find $\frac{1}{8}$)

Percentages

Another way of representing fractions is as a **percentage**. The word 'percentage' comes from 'per centum' meaning 'out of a hundred'. Percentages are used to describe a proportion of a specific group. They are fractions with a denominator of 100. '58% of the class have school dinners' does not imply that the class has

100 children, but simply indicates the proportion of the children having school dinners. It allows for easy comparisons with other classes containing different numbers of children.

The equivalence of fractions, decimals and percentages can be seen if plotted on a number line.

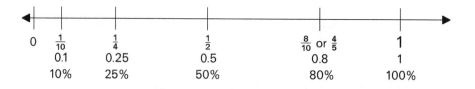

PRACTICAL TASK

What is the VAT on a bicycle costing £250.00? Can you calculate the answer mentally?

Assume that VAT is at 20%. It is useful to know that we can work VAT out mentally by finding 10% and doubling that amount to find 20%. So:

   10% of £250:   £25.00

   Double £25.00:   £50.00 (to find 20%)

Calculating percentages

It is possible to use facts you already know to calculate some percentage problems, such as in the practical task above and the first examples below. Others may require a written method.

To find 15% of 60 it is possible to use a mental method:

   100% = 60

   10% = 6   ($\frac{1}{10}$ of 60)

$5\% = 3 \qquad (\frac{1}{2}$ of 10%)

Giving 15% of $60 = 6 + 3 = 9$

Knowledge of fractions is very useful when calculating some percentages, e.g. to find 75% of 48:

Remember $75\% = \frac{3}{4}$

$\frac{1}{4}$ of $48 = 12$

$\frac{3}{4}$ of $48 = 36$ (12×3)

Hence 75% of $48 = 36$ (because $\frac{3}{4} = 75\%$)

Knowledge of decimals is also useful when calculating percentages. Use the same example as above, to find 75% of 48:

Remember $75\% = 0.75$

$0.75 \times 48 = 36$

Other problems require a pencil and paper calculation, e.g.:

A school has 325 pupils on roll. 64% of these pupils bring a packed lunch to school. How many children have a packed lunch?

In order to answer this, it is necessary to remember that 64% can also be represented by the fraction $\frac{64}{100}$ (remember, percentages are fractions with a denominator of 100). So 64% of 325 can also be written as:

$\dfrac{64}{100} \times 325$

$= \dfrac{64}{4} \times 13$ (dividing 100 and 325 by 25)

$= 16 \times 13$ (dividing 64 and by 4)

$= 208$

Hence, 208 children bring a packed lunch to school.

This can also be answered using the decimal approach. Remember that 64% can be written as:

0.64

0.64 x 325 = 208

Equality

REFLECTIVE TASK

Eles is given the following numbers and expressions and asked to find as many statements about equality as possible. The numbers and expressions given are:

12, 6 + 6, 2 × 6, 24 ÷ 2

The statements she creates are:

$12 = 6 + 6$ $6 + 6 = 12$ $12 = 2 \times 6$ $2 \times 6 = 12$ $12 = 24 \div 2$ $24 \div 2 = 12$

What does this tell you about her understanding of equality?

One thing which is clear is that Eles does understand the symmetric property of equality. However, the transitive property is not yet understood. What subject knowledge do you need to be able to support and extend her knowledge and understanding of equality?

Equality is the mathematical idea which is expressed by the = sign. For example, if 3 is added to 4 then the answer is 7. This can be written as 3 + 4 = 7, the = sign expressing the equality of the two statements.

There are three properties of equality. They are:

- equality is *reflexive*;
- equality is *symmetric*;
- equality is *transitive*.

The **reflexive** property of equality simply means that a = a. For example, 4 = 4 and 627 = 627.

The **symmetric** property of equality can be expressed as 'if $x = y$ then $y = x$'. Eles was showing an understanding of this by recording both $12 = 6 + 6$ and $6 + 6 = 12$.

The **transitive** property means that if $x = y$ and $y = z$ then $x = z$. Using the statements given to Eles, this can be shown as follows:

If $6 + 6 = 12$ and $12 = 24 \div 2$ then $6 + 6 = 24 \div 2$

RESEARCH SUMMARY

Since the 1970s researchers have identified and been considering the effect of children imposing a left-to-right reading of equality statements. This usually becomes ingrained practice so that children become rigid in the way they use these sentences (McNeil and Alibali, 2005) and this can become a significant hurdle to their developing algebraic understanding (Thomas and Tall, 2001). Researchers are now exploring how tasks can encourage children to use commutativity and decomposition (e.g. Carraher et al., 2006; Jones, 2008; Molina et al., 2008) and they are reporting positive findings in relation to children's understanding of the equality sign in more than one rigid way.

Inequalities

An **inequality** simply states that one number is greater or smaller than another. For example, '6 is less than 10' is an inequality and can be written as $6 < 10$. The symbol $<$ means 'less than' when reading left to right. It is also possible to say '10 is greater than 6' which can be written as $10 > 6$. This time the symbol $>$ means 'greater than' when reading left to right. From this it can be seen that $6 < 10$ means the same as $10 > 6$.

Other symbols which may be encountered when dealing with inequalities are $\leq$ which means 'less than or equal to', $\geq$ which means 'greater than or equal to' and $\neq$ which means 'not equal to'. You have already encountered use of the 'not equal to' symbol '$\neq$' when considering the laws of arithmetic.

Inequalities can be manipulated in a similar way to equations. If a number is added to or subtracted from both sides of the inequality, then the inequality is preserved, i.e. the statement is still true, e.g.:

6 < 10

6 + 5 < 10 + 5 (5 is added to each side of the inequality)

11 < 15 (the inequality is preserved, the statement is still true)

Multiplication and division need to be treated slightly differently, depending on whether the number which the inequality is multiplied by, or divided by, is positive or negative.

If an inequality is multiplied or divided by a positive number then the inequality is preserved, e.g.:

6 < 10

$6 \times 2 < 10 \times 2$ (both sides of the inequality are multiplied by 2)

12 < 20 (the inequality is preserved)

And division gives:

6 < 10

$6 \div 2 < 10 \div 2$ (both sides of the inequality are divided by 2)

3 < 5 (the inequality is preserved)

However, if the inequality is multiplied or divided by a negative number then the inequality is reversed, e.g.:

6 < 10

$6 \times -2 < 10 \times -2$

−12 < −20

This is not true. The inequality has been reversed, hence:

−12 > −20

Knowing this, it is possible to reverse the inequality symbol at the appropriate place within the calculation, e.g.:

6 < 10

$6 \div -2 > 10 \div -2$

−3 > −5

Inequalities are frequently encountered within the context of algebra, e.g. $x < 6$ means that x can take any value less than 6. However, if it is written as $x \leq 6$ this means x can take any value less than *or equal to* 6. These can be represented on a number line as:

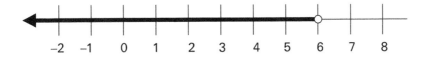

This number line represents $x < 6$. The empty circle at 6 indicates that the value of x cannot be equal to 6.

This number line represents $x \leq 6$. The solid circle at 6 indicates that the value of x can be equal to 6.

Algebraic inequalities can be solved in exactly the same way as algebraic equations more generally. For example, consider $x + 4 > 6$:

$x + 4 > 6$

$x > 6 - 4$ (4 is subtracted from both sides)

$x > 2$

Hence x is greater than 2.

Recurring decimals

REFLECTIVE TASK

Max was asked to calculate a value for $\frac{1}{3}$. The answer given was 0.3.

What does this tell you about his understanding of recurring decimals?

It is clear that Max does not yet understand the conventions for expressing recurring decimals. What subject knowledge do you need to be able to teach him effectively?

Quite frequently in calculations decimal answers arise that go on forever. These are called **recurring decimals**. Examples include:

$$\frac{1}{3} = 0.33333...$$

$$\frac{10}{11} = 0.90909090...$$

In order to record that the decimal recurs without having to write them as above, dots are used to indicate the cycle of digits that is recurring. So the above would more formally be recorded as:

$$\frac{1}{3} = 0.\dot{3} \qquad \frac{10}{11} = 0.\dot{9}\dot{0}$$

This indicates that in the first example the 3 recurs, while in the second example the 90 recurs.

Some recurring decimals have longer cycles of digits recurring, e.g.:

$$\frac{2}{7} = 0.2857142857142...$$

To write this using conventional notation gives:

$$\frac{2}{7} = 0.\dot{2}8571\dot{4}$$ indicating that the cycle of digits 285714 recurs

Recurring decimals form part of a group of numbers known as the **rational numbers**.

Rational and irrational numbers

Recurring decimals form part of the set of rational numbers because they can be written as a fraction. The set of rational numbers includes all numbers that can be written as fractions. This includes all integers, all finite decimals, all recurring decimals, the square roots of perfect squares, e.g. $\sqrt{16}$ and $\sqrt{(\frac{9}{25})}$ and all other vulgar fractions.

Irrational numbers are those numbers that cannot be expressed in fractional form. Such numbers are π and other numbers involving π (for example 6π), roots that cannot be calculated exactly, e.g. $\sqrt{2}$, $\sqrt{5}$, $3\sqrt{7}$, and other numbers involving these roots, e.g. $6 \times \sqrt{2}$. In fact, all square roots other than those of perfect squares are irrational, as are most cube roots.

The set of rational numbers and the set of irrational numbers together make up the **real number** system. Every real number is represented by a point on the number line and conversely, every point on the number line represents a real (i.e. rational or irrational) number. So the number line has no gaps along it.

Index form

REFLECTIVE TASK

Andrew was asked to find an answer for 5^2. The answer that was given was 10.

What does this tell you about his understanding of index form?

It is clear that Andrew does not understand what the index, in this case 2, actually means. What subject knowledge do you need, to be able to extend his understanding of index notation?

Square numbers are the product of two equal factors, e.g. 2×2, 3×3, 4×4.

Cube numbers are the product of three equal factors, e.g. $1 \times 1 \times 1$, $2 \times 2 \times 2$, $3 \times 3 \times 3$.

But what is index form or index notation?

Index form is a concise way of writing multiplication of a number by itself, so $10 \times 10 \times 10 \times 10$ can be written as 10^4.

4 is the **index**
$\downarrow$

10 is the **base** $\longrightarrow$ $10^4 = 10{,}000$ $\longleftarrow$ 10,000 is the 4th **power** of 10
(product of repeated multiplication)

Index form is also frequently encountered within algebraic expressions, e.g. $a^3 \times a^2$. It is interesting to consider what happens to the indices (plural of index) within this multiplication. First it is necessary to consider what the expression actually represents.

$$a^3 \times a^2 = (a \times a \times a)(a \times a)$$
$$= a \times a \times a \times a \times a$$
$$= a^5$$

In effect, the indices have been added.

Consider division:

$$a^6 \div a^3 = \frac{a \times a \times a \times \cancel{a} \times \cancel{a} \times \cancel{a}}{\cancel{a} \times \cancel{a} \times \cancel{a}}$$
$$= a \times a \times a$$
$$= a^3$$

So for division, in effect the indices have been subtracted.

An interesting fact concerning **index notation** – consider the pattern of 'powers of 2'. It could start at $2^1 = 2$, $2^2 = 4$, $2^3 = 8$, $2^4 = 16$ ... But what about 2^0? Any number raised to the power 0 gives the answer 1. Consider why this is the case.

Start with a^3. To move down the sequence to the preceding term it is necessary to divide by a, giving a^2. To move down the sequence again divide by a again, giving a^1. To move down the sequence again to a^0, it is necessary to divide a^1 by a. We already know that $a^1 = a$, so $a^1 \div a = a \div a = 1$. This can be extended into negative powers, a^{-1} being $a^0 \div a = 1 \div a = \frac{1}{a}$.

Look at the pattern in the place value section at the start of Chapter 2 to help you with this.

Standard form

Standard form is sometimes called **standard index form** as it uses powers of 10, i.e. 10 expressed in index form (see above).

Standard form is a shorthand way of writing very small and very large numbers that would require a huge number of digits if written in full. It can be used to express large numbers such as the vast distances of planets from Earth, or small numbers such as the minute scientific measurements within an atom.

In order to express a number in standard form it is written as a number between 1 and 10 then multiplied by a power of 10. The power of 10 is called the **order**

of magnitude and indicates the overall size of the number. The number between 1 and 10 gives greater detail about the overall number. For example:

6000000 written in standard form is 6×10^6

0.0000000759 written in standard form is 7.59×10^{-8}

As can be seen from the above, multiplying by a positive power of 10 gives a number greater than 1, whilst multiplying by a negative power of 10 gives a number less than 1.

It is interesting to note a certain 'symmetry' in the index notation for the powers of 10 used in standard form:

$$1 \text{ is } 10^0 \qquad \frac{1}{1} \text{ is } 10^0$$

$$10 \text{ is } 10^1 \qquad \frac{1}{10} \text{ is } 10^{-1}$$

$$100 \text{ is } 10^2 \qquad \frac{1}{100} \text{ is } 10^{-2}$$

$$1000 \text{ is } 10^3 \qquad \frac{1}{1000} \text{ is } 10^{-3}$$

Ratio and proportion

REFLECTIVE TASK

Neve is asked to identify the proportion of white tiles in the following tiling pattern:

She says 1 in 3 of the tiles is white.

What does this tell you about her understanding of proportion?

It is clear that Neve might be confusing ratio and proportion. What subject knowledge do you need to effectively support and extend this child's knowledge and understanding of ratio and proportion?

Ratio is the comparative size of quantities, numbers or measures of the same kind. It is written either as a:b or as a fraction $\frac{a}{b}$, e.g. 3:5 or $\frac{3}{5}$.

If one bottle holds 200ml and another holds 400ml then the second one is twice as big or they have a ratio of 200:400 or 1:2.

As can be seen in the above example, the ratio of one number to another remains the same if both numbers are multiplied or divided by the same number. This is an **equivalent** ratio.

But this is not the case if numbers are added or subtracted to both numbers, e.g.:

$1:2 \neq 2:3$ and $5:4 \neq 4:3$

Partitioning underlies ratio. For example, if two children shared 7 apples so that child A received 5 apples and child B received 2 apples, their sharing is in a ratio of 5:2.

Child A would receive $\frac{5}{2}$ times more than child B. With more apples to share, child A would always receive 2.5 times as many apples as child B. This demonstrates the multiplicative structure of ratio:

child A	child B
5	2
10	4
15	6
20	8

Ratio can be used to solve other problems, e.g.:

If 5 cakes cost 35p, how much will 3 cakes cost?

Using the ratio 5:3 gives $\frac{5}{3} = \frac{35}{a}$. The value for a can be found by simply rearranging the equation:

$$\frac{5}{3} = \frac{35}{a}$$

$$a = 35 \times \frac{3}{5}$$

$$a = 21$$

So the cost of 3 cakes is 21p.

A **scale factor** can be expressed as a ratio. Imagine Tom has £10 and Joe has £30. In order to have the same amount as Joe, Tom would have to multiply his money by 3, £10 × 3 = £30. The amount has been increased by a scale factor, in this case 1 × 3 or 1:3.

Similarly the ratio structure can be used to **compare** two quantities. An example of this would be the two children, Tom with 20p and Joe with 60p. Joe has 3 times as much money as Tom because 60 ÷ 20 is 3. (Tom's 20p would have to be increased by three to equal Joe's 60p.)

Proportion is sometimes mistakenly used to mean ratio but proportion compares part of a quantity with the whole. So a ratio of 1:3 results in proportions of 1 out of 4 and 3 out of 4. This is the mistake Neve was making.

Imagine a recipe for raisin cup cakes requires 110 g of flour, 60 g of sugar, 100 g of butter, 80 g of raisins and 2 eggs. This recipe will make 12 cakes. How much of each ingredient would be required if 18 cakes were needed? In order to keep the proportions the same, and therefore keep the cakes edible, the ingredients need to be increased in the ratio 18:12 or 3:2. 110 g of flour represents 2 within the ratio 3:2, so to calculate the new value it is necessary to divide by 2, then multiply by 3 giving 165 g. Doing the same for the other ingredients gives: 90 g of sugar, 150 g of butter, 120 g of raisins and 3 eggs.

It is possible to express ratios as percentages (as well as fractions and decimals):

$$2:5 = \frac{2}{5} = 0.4 = \frac{40}{100} = 40\%$$

A SUMMARY OF KEY POINTS

- The use of fractions falls into two main areas, as a measurement and as an operator on another number.

- Decimals form an extension to our place value system.

- Percentages can be considered as another way of representing fractions. They are fractions with a denominator of 100. Percentages can also be represented as decimals.

- Understanding the relationships between decimals, fractions and percentages allows effective and efficient calculations to be undertaken in a range of contexts.

- The set of rational numbers and the set of irrational numbers together make up the real numbers.

- Standard form allows very large and very small numbers to be written concisely.

- Ratio and proportion make use of a multiplicative structure to solve problems.

M-LEVEL EXTENSION

Look at the National Curriculum's requirement around children's learning of fractions in Key Stages 1 and 2 (https://www.gov.uk/government/collections/national-curriculum). Compare these with the requirement of the previous curriculum (http://www.educationengland.org.uk/documents/pdfs/1999-nc-primary-handbook.pdf). Consider how schools have responded to these new requirements. Has your placement school significantly changed their teaching of fractions since 2014? What can we learn from how schools and children have risen to this challenge? Do higher expectations lead to enhanced learning and teaching?

FURTHER READING

DfE (2011) *Teachers' Standards*. Available at https://www.gov.uk/government/uploads/system/uploads/attachment_data/file/301107/Teachers__Standards.pdf

English, R. (2013) *Teaching Arithmetic in Primary Schools*. London: Sage. This text has a strong emphasis on arithmetical understanding. The book is focused on supporting trainees to develop their own subject knowledge. Its friendly writing style supports you to know 'how' to perform many different mathematical procedures, but it also explains how and why these work.

Hansen, A. (2008) *Primary Mathematics: Extending Knowledge in Practice*. Exeter: Learning Matters. This book offers classroom-based case studies that consider some of the most difficult areas of the primary mathematics curriculum to teach.

Thompson, I. (ed.) (2010) *Issues in Teaching Numeracy in Primary Schools*, 2nd edn. Buckingham: Open University Press. This book addresses many issues of current debate within the development of numeracy in schools. It tackles the direct classroom-based issues as well as considering children as learners and how to develop appropriate visual images to support the development of numeracy.

4

Mathematical language, reasoning and proof

Teachers' standards

A teacher must:

3. Demonstrate good subject and curriculum knowledge

    - have a secure knowledge of the relevant subject(s) and curriculum areas, foster and maintain pupils' interest in the subject, and address misunderstandings
    - demonstrate a critical understanding of developments in the subject and curriculum areas, and promote the value of scholarship

4. Plan and teach well structured lessons

    - impart knowledge and develop understanding through effective use of lesson time
    - promote a love of learning and children's intellectual curiosity
    - contribute to the design and provision of an engaging curriculum within the relevant subject area(s)

8. Fulfil wider professional responsibilities

    - take responsibility for improving teaching through appropriate professional development

Curriculum context

Early Years Foundation Stage

In the Early Years Foundation Stage, children solve problems, use everyday language to talk about mathematical ideas, create and describe patterns. Besides being fundamental to the development of algebra, work with pattern introduces the possibility of encouraging children to justify their explanations and predictions, for example by asking questions such as, 'Why do you think we need this shape next?' Children also explore characteristics of everyday objects and shapes and use mathematical language to describe them.

National Curriculum programmes of study

The National Curriculum for mathematics aims to ensure that all pupils:

- become fluent in the fundamentals of mathematics, including through varied and frequent practice with increasingly complex problems over time, so that pupils develop conceptual understanding and the ability to recall and apply knowledge rapidly and accurately.

- reason mathematically by following a line of enquiry, conjecturing relationships and generalisations, and developing an argument, justification or proof using mathematical language.
- can solve problems by applying their mathematics to a variety of routine and non-routine problems with increasing sophistication, including breaking down problems into a series of simpler steps and persevering in seeking solutions.

In the National Curriculum for mathematics the programmes of study clearly state the knowledge, skills and understanding which are to be taught throughout the Key Stages.

At Key Stage 1, in 'Using and applying number, shape, space and measures', there is reference to pupils' explanation and reasoning skills. The importance of these skills as a foundation for proof in later Key Stages is emphasised.

By the end of Upper Key Stage 2, the ability to explain and justify reasoning is taken further and also includes the requirement to develop logical thinking. Pupils might be asked to explain why the 100th term of a number pattern must be a particular value (without, of course, counting all the way up from, say, the 8th term). They could also explore the logical consequences of definitions, such as 'Triangles with two equal sides' and 'Triangles with only two equal sides'.

Mathematical language, reasoning and proof

Introduction

Proof is an essential part of the process of doing mathematics. Although mathematics is often perceived as a tidy, well organised subject, the exploration of mathematical ideas can be quite unstructured and characterised by having hunches, checking, finding oneself up a 'blind alley', trying an alternative strategy and so on. It is at the end of this unpredictable process, when confidence in a generalisation starts to build up, that the aspect of mathematical activity we call proof becomes so important.

Proof is about making certain our ideas are sound. We convince ourselves and justify our results to others. In the classroom, the question 'How do you know it will always happen?' is a starting point for a proof.

Mathematics can be thought of as being rather like a brick wall: concepts build up on other concepts in a connected structure. Mathematicians like to know this 'wall' is in good shape and the bricks are sound. Proof gives this confidence. It makes mathematics neat and tidy. This is why one great mathematician called proof the 'hygiene' of the subject.

It should be emphasised that proof is by no means the preserve of advanced mathematics. The mathematical thinking of pupils at Key Stage 1 and Key Stage 2 should involve proofs, albeit at appropriate levels of sophistication. This might include justifying ideas by pointing out features on diagrams: the so-called informal proofs.

To be able to develop this kind of thinking in the classroom, you first need to understand what is involved in proof. The purpose of the first part of this chapter is to give you this background. The content will also link with aspects of number, algebra and shape elsewhere in this book.

In the second part of the chapter, mathematical language is examined. This includes consideration of the ambiguities in mathematical vocabulary, the development of definitions and mismatches which can occur between language structure and mathematical structure.

Levels of proof

Within the examples from number, shape and measure, there are countless opportunities to develop the idea of proof and the logical thinking which underpins it.

Consider how two groups of primary school children approached thinking about what happens when we add two odd numbers together.

A group of six-year-olds were adding lots of pairs of odd numbers and getting mostly the right answers which they saw were even. After several pages of calculations had been done, the teacher asked the children if they thought the answer would always be even, whichever two odd numbers were added together. The essence of their response was to point to the many calculations showing *odd + odd = even* and to volunteer to do a few extra ones for good measure. They were utterly convinced. It had worked about 30 times so it would always happen!

In the second classroom where the pupils were a little older, the teacher was promoting discussion through the use of a picture to model odd and even numbers. Even numbers were represented by pairs of friends holding hands, while odd numbers were shown as pairs of friends plus one individual standing alone.

Even   Odd

After some practice in making pictures of various odd and even numbers, the teacher led discussion on to what would happen if two odd numbers were added. The children quickly saw that the two unattached children at the end of each line would be able to pair up, thus giving an even number. What is more, it became clear to them that however far the pairs of these odd numbers stretched, the result of putting them together would always be an even number.

Notice the different levels of mathematical thinking in each of these scenarios. In the first example, children are arriving at a generalised rule by trying out a few examples. This type of thinking is known as **induction**. The limitation of the approach is that we can never be sure that the examples we have *not* tried will conform to this rule. The history of mathematics is littered with mathematicians' hunches (conjectures) based on inductive thinking which eventually were shown to be false. An example of this is this pattern of numbers:

31 331 3331 33331 333331 3333331 33333331

Mathematicians knew that the first seven numbers in this pattern were prime (only divisible by one and themselves). They also believed that however long the pattern was continued, the resulting number would be prime. It came as a salutary lesson about the limitations of inductive reasoning when it was discovered that $333333331 = 17 \times 19607843$ and was therefore not prime.

While inductive thinking can often open up exciting possibilities by showing possible relationships, it can never be a guarantee of the validity of these relationships.

Let us now return to the second classroom example. Notice here that the mathematical reasoning is at a much more powerful level. Despite the simple nature of the representation, there was an attempt to justify the general case of addition of **any two** odd numbers. In fact, this 'picture proof is only a short step from a sophisticated algebraic approach. You might find it helpful to reflect on the correspondence between the algebraic proof below and the reasoning based on the pictures.

Proof that the sum of two odd numbers is even:

We can write an even number as 2a, where a is an integer. Similarly, an odd number can be written as 2a + 1. (For example, the odd number 17 is twice 8 plus 1.)

Our two odd numbers could then be 2a + 1 and 2b + 1.

Adding, we have 2a + 1 + 2b + 1

$$= 2a + 2b + 2$$

$$= 2 (a + b + 1)$$

Now a + b + 1 is an integer and this implies that 2(a + b + 1) is even. Therfore the sum of two odd numbers is even.

(Note that 'implies' and 'therefore' could be represented by the symbols => and ∴ respectively.)

The nub of the argument, in more accessible language, is that 2(a + b + 1) is twice some whole number and so must be even.

At this point you may feel confident enough to write an algebraic proof that the sum of two even numbers is even.

We have seen how a simple rule about adding two odd numbers can be justified at different levels ranging from the unsatisfactory inductive approach to the formal algebraic method. This last method is an example of what we call a **deductive proof**. It is effective because, by representing odd and even numbers in a generalised algebraic way, we are taking into account the sums of *all* possible pairs of odd numbers.

Deductive proof

Now we will take a more detailed look at deductive proof.

The proof of the *odd + odd = even* example which we have just considered is characterised by a series of steps. Each step can be **deduced** from the one before. There are also some **assumptions** we have made, for example about the nature of odd and even numbers. We could use the analogy of a ladder to think about deductive proof.

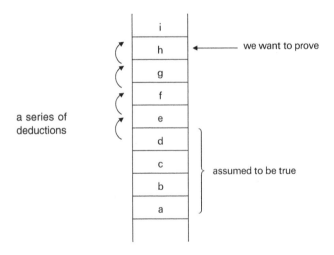

Suppose we want to prove 'idea h' starting from 'idea d'. In starting on rung d, we are taking for granted the ideas a, b, c and d. These have already been proved. They are assumptions. Next we need to logically justify each step up from d to h. It can be thought of as an 'if … then …' process. If d is true, then e must be true; if e is true, then f must be true and so on, finally arriving at 'idea h', which is then proved.

Here is an example of this process in a geometric context:

Proof that the exterior angle of a triangle is equal to the sum of the interior opposite angles:

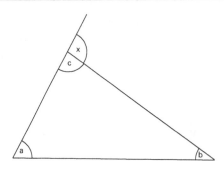

We are trying to prove that, for any triangle, $\hat{x} = \hat{a} + \hat{b}$

We know that $\hat{c} + \hat{x} = 180°$ (a straight angle)

Also, $\hat{c} + \hat{a} + \hat{b} = 180°$ (sum of angles of a triangle)

$\Rightarrow \hat{c} + \hat{x} = \hat{c} + \hat{a} + \hat{b}$

$\therefore \hat{x} = \hat{a} + \hat{b}$

In this short **theorem**, as a geometric proof is sometimes called, we have made some assumptions. It is taken for granted that the sum of the interior angles of a triangle is 180°, and that a straight angle is 180°. Someone else has already proved this. Also, we take as self-evident the rules for manipulating algebraic symbols. From this position on our ladder, we are only two short steps away from our required proof.

Children in primary school are often introduced to the sum of the interior angles of a triangle through the practical exercise of tearing off the angles from paper triangles and fitting these angles together to make half of a rotation:

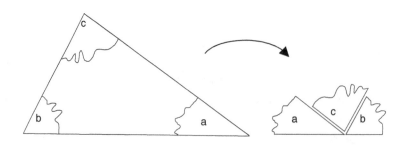

Although the activity lends support to the idea that the sum of the angles might well be 180°, it is not in itself an adequate proof.

PRACTICAL TASK

Try demonstrating that the angles of a quadrilateral total 360 degrees by the same process of tearing off the corners and fitting them together. You could also experiment using pentagons and hexagons, where there would be some 'overlapping' involved.

Proof that the sum of the interior angles of a triangle is 180°:

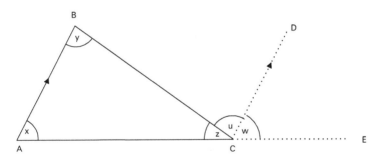

Extend AC to E and draw CD parallel to AB

Hence, the sum of the interior angles of a triangle is 180°.

$\hat{x} = \hat{w}$ (corresponding angles on parallels AB and CD)

$\hat{y} = \hat{u}$ (alternate angles on parallels AB and CD)

Now $\hat{z} + \hat{u} + \hat{w} = 180°$ (straight angle)

Replacing $\hat{u} + \hat{w}$ with $\hat{x} + \hat{y}$,

we have $\hat{z} + \hat{x} + \hat{y} = 180°$

For more information on angles on parallel lines see Chapter 7.

Notice that we are again starting from assumptions, one of which is about the relationship between angles produced when a pair of parallel lines intersects with a third line.

Pythagoras' proof

It is interesting to reflect on the fleeting nature of fame. How many of the names of today's celebrities will have a familiar ring even 50 years from now? In contrast, the Greek mathematician Pythagoras, who lived in the sixth century BCE, has achieved enduring fame.

Pythagoras' theorem states that if the length of the hypotenuse of a right-angled triangle is squared, this is equal to the sum of the squares of the lengths of the two other sides.

For more information on Pythagoras' theorem, see Chapter 7.

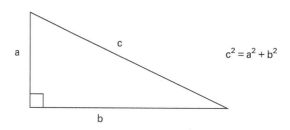

$c^2 = a^2 + b^2$

There are many proofs of Pythagoras' theorem and this is one of the more accessible ones. We start from the assumption that the inner shape shown opposite is a square. This is, in fact, relatively easy to show using the angles of the four right-angled triangles. Also, note that the area of each of the right-angled triangles is $\frac{1}{2}ab$.

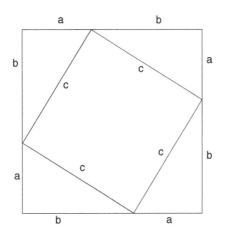

The total area of the large square is (a + b)², but this is equal to the sum of the area of the inner square plus the area of the four right-angled triangles, which is c² + 4($\frac{1}{2}$ab).

Putting these expressions equal to each other gives:

$$\left(a+b\right)^2 = c^2 + 4\left(\tfrac{1}{2}ab\right)$$

Multiplying out the brackets gives:

$$a^2 + 2ab + b^2 = c^2 + 2ab$$

Subtracting 2ab from each side results in:

$$a^2 + b^2 = c^2 \;\; \text{(Pythagoras' relationship)}$$

REFLECTIVE TASK

Our final two examples of deductive proof relate to number. Before reading them it would be beneficial to attempt to prove the results yourself.

Proof that prime numbers greater than three either precede or follow a multiple of six:

(Continued)

83

(Continued)

For example,

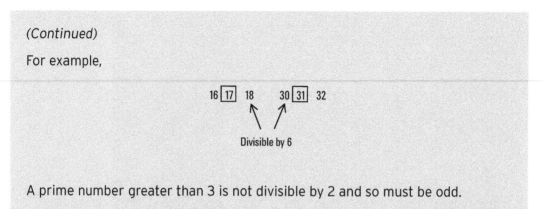

A prime number greater than 3 is not divisible by 2 and so must be odd.

The two numbers either side of the prime must then be even and are divisible by 2.

Any three consecutive numbers must include at least one number which is divisible by 3. This cannot be the central prime number, so it must be one of the two even numbers on either side.

Hence **one** of the numbers either side of a prime is divisible by both 2 and 3 and is therefore divisible by 6. This completes the proof.

Proof that the sum of three consecutive numbers is divisible by 3:

Three consecutive numbers can be expressed as:

n, n+1, n+2

Adding, we have:

$n + n + 1 + n + 2$

$= 3n + 3$

$= 3(n + 1)$ which is divisible by 3.

The converse of a proof

It is important to remember that many logical and mathematical statements have a sense of 'direction' about them. As a simple illustration, the statement 'all cats like milk' does not allow us to infer that 'if something likes milk, it must be a cat'.

Many proofs or theorems are true in both ways. For example 'an equilateral triangle has three equal angles', also works in the opposite direction, and it is true that 'a triangle with three equal angles must be an equilateral triangle'. We call this second statement the **converse** of the first.

An example where the converse is not true is the correct statement 'the diagonals of a kite are perpendicular'. The converse of this statement can be easily refuted by using two sheets of tracing paper to show various possible relationships between two perpendicular lines.

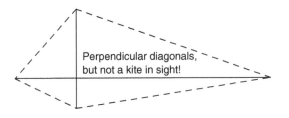

Perpendicular diagonals, but not a kite in sight!

Be on the lookout for proofs for which the converse is false. You might like to consider if the earlier proof that 'the sum of three consecutive numbers is divisible by 3' has a converse.

The steps of an algebraic proof, in which symbols are added and multiplied then regrouped, are based on the fundamental laws of arithmetic, which we assume to be true. These laws include the **commutative**, **associative** and **distributive relationships** and rules about inverses. For example, we take for granted that $2a + 2b$ can be changed to $2(a + b)$. When we switch on our 'rules of algebra autopilot', some interesting consequences emerge.

For more information on these laws, see the section on laws of arithmetic in Chapter 2.

It is easy to make a plausible case for the answer to $+2 \times -3$. Writing two cheques each for £3 results in a debit of £6, i.e. -6. In a similar way, the calculation could have been modelled using two temperature reductions of three degrees each. Why is it then that $-2 \times -3 = +6$? More support is needed than the famous 'two minuses make a plus', and children often find it perplexing that there is no helpful everyday justification for this result. The reason why $-2 \times -3 = +6$ is found in the rules of arithmetic, rather than our everyday world.

Let us assume the result $+2 \times -3 = -6$ (we could prove this in a similar way)

Let $-2 \times -3 = y$

adding $+2 \times -3$ to each side we have:

$$+2 \times -3 + -2 \times -3 = +2 \times -3 + y$$

factorising the left-hand side gives:

$$-3(+2 + -2) = +2 \times -3 + y$$

So $\qquad -3(0) = -6 + y$

And $\qquad 0 = -6 + y$

$\therefore \qquad y = +6$

If the rules of arithmetic are consistent for both positive and negative numbers, then -2×-3 *must* equal $+6$.

We now move on to consider two other types of proof which are part of a mathematician's armoury.

Disproof by counter-example

An advantage of this type of proof is that it is usually much easier to prove something is not true than prove that it is true. The statement 'all Englishmen like cricket' would be extremely difficult to verify. Even if we had knocked on every door in the land and all the replies had been affirmative, there would still be a niggling doubt that we might have missed someone. To disprove this assertion would only require one Englishman to say he did not like cricket. It might take a while to find him but, once done, the disproof would be complete.

Our 'Englishman who does not like cricket' is known as a **counter-example**. Finding counter-examples is a powerful way of disproving assertions and is a useful technique for encouraging children to reflect on misconceptions.

An example of such an interaction which might encourage a child to reflect on the definition of a square could be:

(Teacher)   Tell me how you know if a shape is a square.

(Child)   It has got four sides all the same length.

(T)   So this is a square then:

(C)   Oh, it's not...

Here is a geometric example of the use of counter-example. The figure opposite shows various numbers of dots marked on the circumference of circles and joined up to form regions.

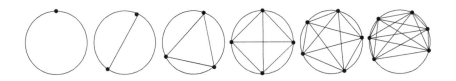

Counting the regions in the first four circles gives the numbers 1, 2, 4 and 8. At this point a mathematician's pulse starts to race a little. Will the next circle have 16 regions? Sure enough it has. Excitement really sets in as the regions are counted for the sixth circle. Hopes are dashed though, as recounting verifies that the number of regions is in fact 31 and not the expected 32. This is the counter-example which proves that we are not dealing with a simple doubling relationship. In fact the formula relating dots and regions is as follows:

$$\frac{1}{24}(n^4 - 6n^3 + 23n^2 - 18n + 24)$$

'When a number is multiplied by 10, a nought is added' is a commonly generalised rule. It is true for multiplying whole numbers by ten, but a counter-example such as 0.2×10 highlights its limited validity.

In the context of measurement, younger children frequently make a gener-alisation based on their experience that bigger objects are heavier than smaller objects. It seems quite reasonable to them as, after all, footballs are heavier than tennis balls. A large block of polystyrene is an appropriate counter-example to demolish this incorrect assertion.

We have seen how counter-examples are not only important in refuting incorrect conjectures, but can also be a powerful teaching strategy for encouraging chil-dren to reflect on and refine their mathematical beliefs.

There is an old adage: the exception proves the rule. In mathematics, however, it is the exception which disproves the rule.

PRACTICAL TASK

This classroom example provides children with an opportunity to appreciate the value of counter-examples.

(Continued)

(Continued)

One child devises a rule for a sequence of four digits which is kept secret from the others in the group. They are, however, given one example which fits the rule. This could be, for example:

7 5 3 1

The group then tries to discover the secret rule by suggesting other examples, which receive the answer yes or no according to whether they fit or not.

There are many possible rules which could accommodate this particular four-digit sequence. Here are some of them:

a)   descending list of consecutive odd numbers;

b)   a descending list of odd numbers;

c)   any four-digit list;

d)   a number less than 10000;

e)   a list of four or fewer odd digits.

Suppose the secret rule chosen was e). Which examples would help the group 'home in' on it? Clearly 9 7 5 3 would not provide a counter-example for any of the rules a) to e). Suggesting 5 3 1 though would enable c) to be rejected. Certainly 1 9 7 would be a useful example to present. Why?

A key aspect of this activity is to encourage children to choose their counter-examples carefully.

Try inventing some other rules for digit sequences and appropriate counter-examples.

Proof by exhaustion

The general proofs considered earlier in this chapter take into account the infinite nature of our number system and the countless number of shapes which could be drawn. These proofs ensure we do not have to check, one by one, all the possible pairs of odd numbers or all the different types of triangles. Indeed, this would be impossible, not because of the time factor or effort involved, but in principle.

There are, however, occasions when a convincing proof can be arrived at by considering all the possibilities. This approach is known as **proof by exhaustion**. Here are some examples:

Proof that there are eight possible outcomes if you toss a coin three times.

This can be shown easily with the help of a tree diagram:

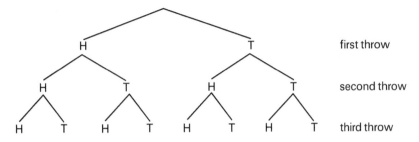

Following every route from top to bottom gives the eight possibilities.

The following activity involves combining moves about a network. The four moves are horizontal (H), vertical (V), diagonal (D) and no move (N). We always start or finish on a corner of the rectangle.

Proof that if we 'add' any pair of moves the system is closed (i.e. we only get answers which are in the original set of moves):

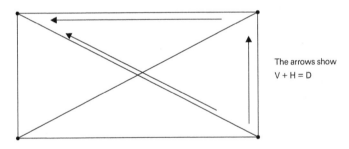

The arrows show
V + H = D

The possibilities can be exhausted by setting out an 'addition' table where V + H means, 'V followed by H':

+	N	H	V	D
N	N	H	V	D
H	H	N	D	V
V	V	D	N	H
D	D	V	H	N

It can be seen that the addition of any pair of moves results in one of the four original moves. The symmetry of the network makes it irrelevant which corner we start from.

(This is an example of what is known in mathematics as a **finite group**.)

It is important, when exhausting possibilities, to work systematically. Children, left to their own devices, frequently work in a haphazard manner which can result in omissions. They are left wondering, 'Have I got them all?'

The next example requires an exhaustive search.

Proof that six different tiles can be made using one colour to shade in the triangles in the following shape:

The first point to note is that there will be some duplicate patterns, for example:

 is the same as

By colouring first none, then one, then two, then three and finally all the triangles, we have the confirmation that the six possibilities are:

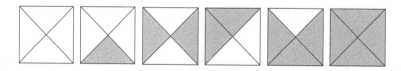

Using different shapes, it is possible to devise many variants of this activity. One example would be to start with a 3 by 2 grid and colour various numbers of squares.

Nets which fold up to make solid shapes offer possibilities for exhaustive searches. As you will see in Chapter 7, there are 11 ways in which six squares can be joined together to form the net of a cube. Finding them requires a systematic approach.

Asking children to exhaustively prove they have considered all possibilities involves them in organising and checking their work.

Not all exhaustive methods are as straightforward as finding the nets of a cube. In 1852, mathematician Francis Guthrie was colouring in a map showing the counties of England, when it occurred to him that there might be a rule for the minimum number of colours required for any map, so that the same colour was not used on either side of a common border. He found he needed only four colours. For over 100 years, no one could find a map that needed more than four colours, yet mathematicians were unable to prove this. It became known as the **four-colour problem**. In 1976, Haken and Appel reduced the problem to 1482 basic configurations and used a computer to check all the combinations within these maps. After 1200 hours of computer running time, it was found that none had required more than four colours. This so-called 'silicon proof' caused consternation among some mathematicians because it was humanly impossible to check what had taken a computer so long to do; on the other hand, they were reluctant to take the result on trust from a machine.

Knowledge of the following two types of proof is not essential for QTS status. They are included for interest and also to give a more complete overview of this important aspect of mathematical activity.

Reductio ad absurdum

This type of proof involves assuming that an idea which is in doubt is actually true. Working with this assumed truth, a contradiction arises which confirms the original belief. The easiest approach to understanding this is through an example.

It is interesting to ask adults and children the answer to dividing a number by zero, e.g. $6 \div 0$. Answers such as 0, 6 or even infinity (note there is no number called infinity) are sometimes given. Younger children often reason along the lines: 'There are 6 sweets and nobody is there to share them, so there will be 6 left.' The correct answer to this problem is that it is impossible to divide by zero. If we try, contradictions emerge.

Proof that we cannot divide by zero:

Let us assume that division by zero is possible. The consequence of this is that zero must behave like other numbers, e.g.:

$$1 \div 1 = 1, 5 \div 5 = 1, 37 \div 37 = 1, x \div x = 1 \text{ so } 0 \div 0 = 1$$

Now $2 \times 0 = 3 \times 0 = 0$

Dividing by zero gives:

$$\frac{2\times0}{0}=\frac{3\times0}{0}$$

Cancelling the zeros,

$$\frac{2\times\cancel{0}}{\cancel{0}}=\frac{3\times\cancel{0}}{\cancel{0}}$$

$$\therefore 2=3$$

This is clearly absurd. Hence, we cannot divide by zero.

Euclid, the Greek mathematician who lived 250 years after Pythagoras, used this sophisticated technique to prove the existence of the irrational numbers.

Proof by induction

This technique should not be confused with inductive thinking, in which generalisations are made from a limited number of examples.

One way of arriving at a plausible rule for the sum of the first n natural numbers is to take the list, reverse it and add the two together:

For example:
$$\begin{array}{ll} & 1+2+3+4 \\ + & 4+3+2+1 \\ \hline & 5+5+5+5 \end{array} \qquad \begin{array}{ll} & 1+2+3+4+5+6 \\ + & 6+5+4+3+2+1 \\ \hline & 7+7+7+7+7+7 \end{array}$$

Finally, we halve each total and arrive at the sum:

$$\frac{4\times5}{2}=10 \text{ and } \frac{6\times7}{2}=21$$

Doing this for several lists suggests the formula:

$$\frac{1}{2}n(n+1)$$

We can check that this formula works for particular lists, but how can we be sure it must always give the correct sum, however long the list of numbers?

The following analogy will help convey a sense of what is involved in this proof. An interesting spectacle is provided by lining up, in patterns, hundreds of dominoes with each one standing on its end. The first domino can be pushed over which starts a ripple travelling down the line until the last shape falls over. If it were possible to line up an infinite number of dominoes, this ripple would go on for ever. What conditions would ensure that all the dominoes go over?

(1) If any domino falls, the one after it must fall.

(2) The first domino falls over.

These two conditions are the basis of proof by induction.

Proof that the formula for the first n natural numbers is given by:

$$\frac{1}{2}n(n+1)$$

We first assume the formula is true for n and demonstrate that it must therefore be true for n + 1. This is equivalent to changing the above formula to:

$$\frac{1}{2}(n+1)\big[(n+1)+1\big]$$

$$\left(\text{Like going from } \frac{1}{2} \text{ of } 6\times7 \text{ to } \frac{1}{2} \text{ of } 7\times8.\right)$$

Assume $\text{sum}(n) = \frac{1}{2}n(n+1)$

Then $\text{sum}(n+1) = \text{sum}(n)+(n+1)$

$\text{sum}(n+1) \quad = \frac{1}{2}n(n+1)+(n+1)$

Rearranging and regrouping gives:

$$\text{sum}(n+1) = \frac{n(n+1)+2(n+1)}{2}$$

$$= \frac{1}{2}(n+1)(n+2)$$

$$\therefore \text{sum}(n+1) = \frac{1}{2}(n+1)\big[(n+1)+1\big]$$

Note that this is the original formula with n + 1 replacing n. We have shown condition (1) applies.

Finally, all we have to address is condition (2), that the formula works for the first natural number, one.

$$\text{sum}(1) = \frac{1}{2} \times 1 \times (1+1) = 1 \text{ completing the proof}$$

So, the first domino falls over and the rest follow one by one for ever.

Mathematical proof versus scientific theories

Mathematicians have devised sophisticated techniques of proof to underpin their ideas with certainty. Starting from assumptions, the truth of which has been established, they argue step by step to a new conclusion. If the argument is logically sound, then the conclusion is established for all time. The theorems of Euclid and Pythagoras are as true today as they were 2000 years ago and another two millennia are unlikely to dent their validity.

This is not the case with scientific theories which are the poor relations of mathematical proofs. In science, hypotheses are suggested as likely explanations of the physical world. If the hypothesis is sound, then further observations will strengthen our belief in it. The hypothesis enables us to make predictions which can be tested and further increase our confidence. As more and more evidence accumulates, our confidence in the hypothesis reaches the point where it becomes known as a theory.

Theories, however, unlike proofs, have a potential 'shelf life' and are the best explanations of the world only until someone comes along with a better idea.

Theories are subjected to the evolutionary pressures of competition and only the fittest survive. There is an enormous graveyard of scientific theories, including some which, in their time, were outstanding. Even Newton's towering achievements have been found inadequate to explain what happens at extremes of size and velocity. Quantum physics and Einstein's General Theory of Relativity have taken over as better explanations of what happens at sub-atomic levels and in the depths of our universe.

The four-colour problem was an indication that mathematical proofs can be long and intractable. Perhaps the most famous example of a difficult proof is the one originating with Pierre de Fermat. It came to be known as **Fermat's Last Theorem**.

For more information on Pythagorean triples, see section on Pythagoras' theorem in Chapter 7.

Fermat, who lived in France in the seventeenth century, was a prodigiously talented mathematician. The starting point of his theorem was the whole-number solutions to Pythagoras' Theorem, the so-called **Pythagorean triples**, examples of which are:

3, 4, 5 $(3^2 + 4^2 = 5^2)$ and 5, 12, 13 $(5^2 + 12^2 = 13^2)$

These examples demonstrate that there are whole numbers, a, b and c which satisfy the equation:

$a^2 + b^2 = c^2$

Fermat then pondered whether there might be whole number solutions for higher powers of a, b and c in equations such as:

$a^3 + b^3 = c^3$

$a^4 + b^4 = c^4$

Although it was known that there is an infinite number of Pythagorean triples, no solutions to the equations for higher powers of a, b and c could be found. After Fermat's death, his collected notes indicated that he had devised a short proof that there were no whole-number solutions for $z > 2$ for the equation:

$a^z + b^z = c^z$

Unfortunately, this proof never came to light and the problem tantalised mathematicians for 350 years. Although it kept the title of 'theorem', it should really have been known as Fermat's Conjecture, as no proof was available. Finally, in 1995, after numerous attempts by mathematicians over many years, Andrew Wiles of Cambridge solved Fermat's Last Theorem. Whether Fermat did devise a short, valid proof is uncertain. It could be an interesting case of achieving lasting fame for failing to prove a theorem!

The outlining of various ways of proof might have left the impression that mathematical reasoning is used only when important mathematical relationships are verified. This is not the case. Mathematical reasoning should permeate mathematical activity across all the curriculum stages.

Language in mathematics

A cursory glance at the language of mathematics confirms there are many potential difficulties and ambiguities. Even the most exotic of flowers is unlikely to have a square root, while 'take-aways' in the mathematics classroom do not usually come topped with pepperoni! In this section we explore some of these issues.

The concepts which are the building blocks of mathematics are abstract and therefore lack physical reality. We can have three chairs, three biscuits and three pencils. These can be seen and touched. Three on its own, however, has no concrete reality. It is a generalisation. In order to think about mathematics ourselves and talk about it with others, we need a means of representing these subtle and often difficult ideas.

There are three ways in which we can represent mathematical ideas.

First, they can be described using words, phrases and sentences. For example, 'quadrilateral', 'which are factors of 12' and 'multiply each side of the equation by 3' each say something mathematical.

The second representation is through the use of pictures and objects, which can be a valuable aid to understanding. Younger children particularly benefit from representations such as **number lines** and **tens/units apparatus**. These help develop images which can then be internalised. There is a saying that a picture paints a thousand words and many people find, for example, the grid representation of long multiplication very helpful in clarifying understanding. Though these concrete props are useful, mathematics is a mental activity, and children should not be using apparatus indiscriminately once understanding has become secure.

A problem can arise when certain representations are exclusively linked with particular aspects of mathematics. For example, it is sometimes forgotten that fractions should appear on the number line and not just as parts of circles or squares.

Third, and most challenging for children, is the use of symbols to represent mathematics. Because of their abstract nature, symbols are introduced after the use of language and pictorial representation. The premature introduction of symbolism can be a barrier to understanding and confidence. It would be impossible to develop mathematically without familiarity with symbols, and teachers have to make fine judgements about the right moment to take this step. The relationship between these three representations of mathematical ideas can be shown as:

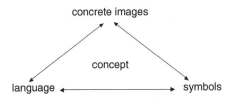

For example, taking the idea of place value, there could be links between:

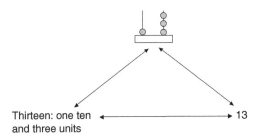

The remainder of this chapter will focus on the use of language to describe mathematical ideas.

Vocabulary

Difficult mathematical language has tended to be pruned from the curriculum over recent years and few children have to grapple with words like *subtrahend* and *quotient*. There is, however, a basic repertoire of precise terms which are a necessary part of mathematical education. Terms such as *numerator* and *denominator* need to be learned. Descriptions such as 'the number at the top' are not only more complicated but also vague and apply to a range of very different mathematical examples. A well-meaning but misguided tendency to avoid what are considered difficult words also fails to take into account that these terms are no more complicated than words such as *refrigerator* or *computer*.

Besides technical terms, used exclusively within a mathematical context, there are many words which have a meaning both within mathematics and also in everyday usage. Sometimes the everyday meaning coincides with the mathematical meaning, but on other occasions the meanings are quite different, causing problems for children. The terms *Ordinary English (OE)* and *Mathematical English (ME)* were coined to draw attention to the complex interplay between language and mathematics. The table below shows examples of these different categories:

Perhaps you can think of other vocabulary to add to these lists.

ME same as OE	ME different from OE	A ME meaning only
Price	Difference	Equilateral
Twelve	Match	Isosceles
Wide	Odd	Parallelogram
Cube	Mean	Numerator
Oblong	Power	Hypotenuse
Vertical	Table	Rhombus
Clockwise	Volume	Subtract
	Product	Congruent
	Cancel	
	Factor	

Words with just a mathematical meaning can be difficult for children. Much of this vocabulary has Latin and Greek origins and children are unlikely to have any background from which useful connections can be made. Another factor is that children simply do not hear these words frequently enough in context, and so familiarity is slow to develop.

Words which have different meanings in OE and ME cause much confusion and it is often only by probing that these difficulties come to light. The attempt by children to make sense of wrong meanings such as odd (peculiar) numbers is both interesting and illuminating.

In order to avoid ambiguity and develop correct terminology, it is important that teachers are aware of the need to discuss these differences in meaning. Straker (1993) stresses the need to extend informal vocabulary by gradually refining terms to give more precise meaning. Each child should trace steps from the familiar to the new. The implication here is that there should be progression in the development of mathematical language and this should be reflected in school planning. In sorting out a suitable order in which to introduce mathematical concepts, it is easy to forget that the development of language such as:

three fours, three times four, three lots of four, three multiplied by four, and the product of three and four,

should be in well-planned stages.

Refining definitions

Before focusing on mathematical definitions, it will be helpful to consider how meaning becomes attached to an everyday word like **car**.

Imagine a young child's first encounter with a car: it could be the red one in the drive. Soon, however, all sorts of other objects are associated with the label 'car'. There is the blue one next door and the grey one across the road. Gradually, many slightly different looking objects are associated with car, even the scale model toys which arrive on birthdays. Alongside this, the child learns about things which are not cars: the machine on two wheels is a bicycle, while the four-wheeled vehicle, which looks like a car with a large matchbox on the back, is not a car but a lorry.

Though a crude simplification, this story illustrates some important points. In learning about a definition, it helps to:

• associate the definition with different examples – the more varied, the better;
• see examples which, though looking vaguely related, do not fit the definition.

The parents of this hypothetical child do not have to arrange for all the vehicles to pull up outside their house so they can point and say 'car', 'car', 'car', 'lorry', etc. Everyday life will take care of this and the frequent encounters with a variety of 'cars' and 'not cars' will ensure the definition is refined.

The way children learn about definitions such as 'triangle' and 'half' could proceed in a similar way, except that everyday life is not littered with a varied range of examples of 'triangles' and 'halves'. Children have to rely mainly on teachers and motivated parents to offer this experience. To develop a clear notion of what triangles and halves are, pupils need to experience, over time, triangles of all shapes and sizes, and halves that are not limited to straight lines drawn across symmetrical shapes.

As well as examples which match the definitions, counter-examples which hint at inclusion are also of crucial importance. It is by linking vocabulary with carefully chosen examples that teaching misconceptions can often be avoided.

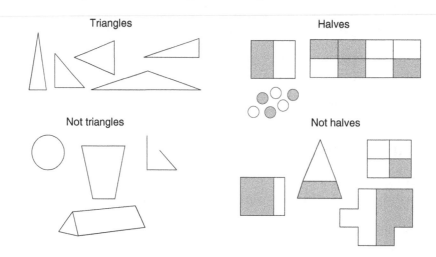

Structure in mathematics and language

Though language patterns and mathematical structure can mirror each other, there are many occasions of mismatch between them. For example, consider the problem:

There are 16 people at a party. Five more arrive. How many are there at the party now?

The language pattern corresponds well with the probable method of calculation, in which 5 is added to 16, and also with the symbolic form, $16 + 5 = \square$.

On the other hand, a problem like:

After putting £6 into my account, I now have £32. How much did I have in my account before this transaction?

shows a much weaker match between the language pattern and the mathematical calculation, $\square + 6 = 32$. Neither the sequencing of the events referred to in the sentence nor the ordering of the numbers corresponds with the standard form of the calculation.

In order to explain the variety of ways of describing addition and subtraction relationships, we can consider the range of problems which involve the numbers 3, 4 and 7:

What is 3 add 4?

What is the total of 3 and 4?

What is 7 take away 3?

What is the difference between 7 and 4?

How many more is 7 than 3?

How many less than 7 is 3?

If 3 is subtracted from 7, what do we get?

What added to 4 makes 7?

I took 4 from a number and got 3. What was the number?

The connection between these problems and the standard forms for addition and subtraction is far from straightforward. Not surprisingly, younger children frequently approach, 'How many more is 7 than 3?', by adding 7 and 3 together to get 10.

Children can become familiar with problem patterns by discussing the meaning and representing them in a concrete context such as a number line or money. Varying the numbers in the problem can also be a way of creating 'tension' between the mathematical structure and the language structure. Here is an example:

Problem: What do you add to 18 to get 25?

Child   (C):   7

Teacher (T):   How did you do it?

          (C):   I counted 19, 20, 21, 22, 23, 24, 25 and that's 7.

          (T):   Good. Can you think of another way of working it out?

          (C):   No.

          (T):   Let's try a different one. What do you add to 2 to get 25?

          (C):   23

          (T):   That was quick. Did you count up from 2 to 25?

          (C):   No, I took away 2.

          (T):   What made you think of doing that?

          (C):   Oh, there's two ways, but counting up takes too long.

The key features of this example are that, while the language in the problem encourages a 'count on' approach, the coupling of a very small number with 25 cries out for the subtraction method. This tension results in a new strategy.

Note that the problem, '25 takeaway 24', encourages a 'count on' strategy. This approach is extremely valuable in clarifying the inverse relationship.

The number system

There are many inconsistencies in the way the number words are said, causing difficulties for many children. In order to see the irregularities of the English system, it is helpful to compare it with the Chinese structure of naming numbers. The Chinese words are translated into English for easy reading.

English	Chinese
One	One
Two	Two
Three	Three
Four	Four
Five	Five
Six	Six
Seven	Seven
Eight	Eight
Nine	Nine
Ten	Ten
Eleven	Ten one
Twelve	Ten two
Thirteen	Ten three
...	...
Eighteen	Ten eight
Nineteen	Ten nine
Twenty	Two ten
Twenty-one	Two ten one
Twenty-two	Two ten two
...	...
Twenty-nine	Two ten nine

Thirty	Three ten
...	...
Eighty	Eight ten
Ninety	Nine ten
One hundred	One hundred
One hundred and one	One hundred one

What is immediately striking about the Chinese system is its regularity. Having learned the first twelve words and 'two ten' it is easy to construct the whole pattern from one to 100 and beyond. Several Asian languages, including Japanese, have this same logical structure.

The English system has features which make it more difficult to discern the underlying tens–units pattern:

- the words eleven and twelve do not indicate a 'ten and' composition;
- the words 'three' and 'five' are not used again (other than to indicate units), but occur in the form 'thir'(teen) and 'fif'(teen);
- in the 'teens' words, the tens and units are reversed (sixteen not teen six);
- 'teen' and 'ty' both mean ten;
- 'twenty' does not clearly indicate two tens.

It is not surprising then that children sometimes reverse the digits in 'thirteen'.

Other European languages such as French and German have some of the same problems as our own system. The French system, having roughly matched our own structure to sixteen, suddenly becomes *dix-sept* for seventeen. The later decades are different with 80 being *quatre-vingt* (four twenties). The German system has not only the 'teens' reversed but also higher numbers like *vierund-zwanzig* (24) which reads like the number words in 'four and twenty blackbirds, baked in a pie'.

The way we say numbers includes several interesting features. The number 234 is read 'two hundred and thirty-four', with the most significant digit (i.e. the hundreds) being articulated first. Thompson (1997) found that 87% of children preferred to perform addition calculations in the same left-to-right manner, starting with the most significant digit first.

We read large numbers in a variety of different ways. 1066 could be expressed as:

'One thousand and sixty-six.'

On the other hand, if the Battle of Hastings was being referred to it would certainly become:

'Ten sixty-six.'

Yet again, as a telephone number it might be:

'One, zero, double six.'

When we read a decimal number such as 34.34, the digits following the decimal point are articulated differently from the ones to the left of the point:

'Thirty-four point three four'.

A SUMMARY OF KEY POINTS

- Proofs are techniques used to convince oneself and others that mathematical ideas are valid. Unlike inductive thinking, which relies on a limited number of cases, proofs are general and apply to all examples.
- There are several standard methods of proof including: deductive proof, characterised by logical, step-by-step justification; disproof by counter-example, in which an argument is refuted by producing a case which does not fit the rule; and proof by exhaustion, in which all possibilities are checked.
- Mathematics is a hierarchical body of knowledge. At whatever level they are engaged, mathematicians need to know that their work rests on firm foundations. Proof gives this guarantee.
- Proof is important at all stages of mathematics education. Primary school children should be taught to reflect on and justify their reasoning, so laying a foundation for more formal approaches to proof in the later key stages.
- Language is one of three ways of representing mathematics.
- Key mathematical vocabulary is important and children need to become familiar with precise terminology.

- Mathematical vocabulary can have a different meaning in ordinary English. These differences should be made explicit to children.

- Children's informal vocabulary should be gradually refined into a more precise meaning. Part of this process will involve discussion of well-chosen exemplars.

- Language structure and mathematical structure sometimes do not match well. Children need to practise linking verbal problems with familiar contexts. The choice of numbers can affect the way the problem is perceived.

- Our number system has many inconsistencies which can be a hindrance to children learning the number names.

M-LEVEL EXTENSION

When observing mathematics lessons, try to identify when children are being encouraged to reason logically. It could be, for example, in explaining why a particular calculation works or why a number pattern enables them to make predictions.

When planning your own mathematics lessons, think of ways in which you might expect children to use mathematical reasoning. It might be, for example, in designing questions which require children to justify a mathematical idea to you and also to other children. While doing this, it would be useful to refer to the Further Reading suggestions below.

When planning, be clear about progression in the introduction of new terminology over a series of lessons. For example, in learning about length, in what order should terms such as 'long', 'tall' and 'high' be introduced and how could they be 'connected up' for children? Would it be useful to include new mathematical vocabulary in your regular lists of spellings for tests, or would this be confusing, as highlighted for some ME words earlier in this chapter?

FURTHER READING

DfE (2011) *Teachers' Standards*. Available at https://www.gov.uk/government/uploads/system/uploads/attachment_data/file/301107/Teachers__Standards.pdf

DfES (2000) *Mathematical Vocabulary*. London: DfES.

Durkin, K. and Shire, B (eds) (1991) *Language in Mathematical Education, Research and Practice*. Buckingham: Open University Press.

Haylock, D. (2014) *Mathematics Explained for Primary Teachers*, 5th edn. London: Sage.

Mason, J., Burton, L. and Stacey, K. (2010) *Thinking Mathematically*, revised edn. Harlow: Pearson.

Ofsted (2007) *Mathematics: Understanding the Score – Improving Practice in Mathematics Teaching at Primary Level*. London: Ofsted.

Thompson, I. (ed.) (2010) *Issues in Teaching Numeracy in Primary Schools*, 2nd edn. Buckingham: Open University Press.

5

Algebra, equations, functions and graphs

Teachers' Standards

A teacher must:

3. Demonstrate good subject and curriculum knowledge

    - have a secure knowledge of the relevant subject(s) and curriculum areas, foster and maintain pupils' interest in the subject, and address misunderstandings
    - demonstrate a critical understanding of developments in the subject and curriculum areas, and promote the value of scholarship

4. Plan and teach well structured lessons

    - impart knowledge and develop understanding through effective use of lesson time
    - promote a love of learning and children's intellectual curiosity
    - contribute to the design and provision of an engaging curriculum within the relevant subject area(s)

8. Fulfil wider professional responsibilities

    - take responsibility for improving teaching through appropriate professional development

Curriculum context

Early Years Foundation Stage

The Early Years Foundation Stage recognises the importance of certain key skills in mathematical development. The areas identified include knowing and using numbers, knowing shapes and solving mathematical problems. This encourages an early introduction to algebra as patterning as well as leading eventually into the specific areas of equations, functions and graphs.

National Curriculum programmes of study

The Mathematics National Curriculum clearly states the knowledge, skills and understanding which are to be taught throughout the key stages.

At Key Stage 1, children develop their ability to recognise, describe, draw, compare and sort different shapes and use the related vocabulary.

At Lower Key Stage 2, children develop mathematical reasoning and confidently describe relationships between numbers and shapes.

After a sound foundation in arithmetic, Upper Key Stage 2 children are introduced to the language of algebra as a means for solving a variety of problems.

Algebra, equations, functions and graphs

Introduction

REFLECTIVE TASK

Before beginning this chapter, take time to consider what 'algebra' actually means. Make a list of any words, phases or ideas you associate with algebra. Your list will be informed by your previous mathematical experiences. If you had a positive time learning maths then your list will reflect this with possible mention of patterns and relationships. If your previous learning was less positive then you might be more aware of the manipulation of symbols and less aware of the uses of algebra.

'Algebra' is a word that is frequently misunderstood or even feared. So, what is algebra? It is certainly about the manipulation of symbols, but that is only a small part, at the very end of the mathematical thinking. Before the symbols come the patterns – seeing, interpreting and expressing patterns is at the heart of algebra. How the patterns are expressed eventually leads to the symbolic form, having passed through diagrams or pictures and words. Representing these patterns symbolically leads to the study of equations and functions, and representing these equations and functions leads to graphing. An understanding of equations, functions and graphs is very important as it allows us to represent some aspects of mathematics in a clear and concise way. By using unknowns to write an equation, or within a function, it is possible to see the range of answers easily from one statement. Equally, representing the **data** as a graph allows trends to be identified and information to be interpreted from a visual image, which is often a lot more straightforward than looking solely at the numbers.

RESEARCH SUMMARY

Carpenter and Levi (2000) conducted a number of studies looking at developing algebraic reasoning in primary-aged children. They based their studies on the premise *that the artificial separation of arithmetic and algebra deprives students of powerful schemes for thinking about mathematics in the early grades and makes it more difficult for them to learn algebra in the later grades.* If it is accepted that understanding of mathematical concepts takes a long time to develop, then algebraic thinking must be conceived as developing over an extended period of time starting in the early primary years. They are adamant that in order to address this developing understanding successfully the current secondary school algebra curriculum should not simply be pushed down into primary schools. They have a much broader conception of the nature of algebra in which the emphasis is not simply on learning rules for manipulating symbols. The goal is for children to develop algebraic thinking, not solely the skilled use of algebra procedures.

Their research looked at primary children over a period of time as they explore the nature of equality and justify conjectures. Overall, they found that children in the primary grades can engage in formulating, representing and justifying conjectures. They did also conclude, however, that primary children tend to value examples, sometimes multiple examples, over principled explanations to validate the conjectures they are capable of identifying.

The area of mathematics known as algebra derives its name from a book entitled *Hisab al-jabr wa'l muqabalah* by Muhammad al-Khwarizmi (c.780–c.850). The title translates as 'Calculation by *Restoration* and *Reduction*'. **Restoration** means simplifying an equation by performing the same operation on each side and *reduction* involves combining different parts of the equation to make it simpler. Muhammad al-Khwarizmi's ideas have been so influential in the world of mathematics that the word *al-jabr* in the title of his book has become the *algebra* of today.

Although Muhammad al-Khwarizmi has been extremely influential in the area of algebra, the ideas have been known about since ancient Egyptian times. The Rhind Papyrus is named after the Scottish Egyptologist Alexander Henry Rhind who acquired it in 1858. It is also sometimes called the Ahmes Papyrus after the scribe who wrote it in about 1650 BCE. He stated that it was copied from an even earlier document of around 2000 BCE. It is now kept in the British Museum. This papyrus contains the first documentary evidence of the use of algebra. Unknowns are represented as symbols within simple problems for solving. Compared to algebra today it is very basic, but it is important to remember that the knowledge and understanding of today has been built up over a considerable amount of time from foundations like the Rhind Papyrus.

Algebraic expressions

REFLECTIVE TASK

As the result of an investigation in class, Zoe and David establish the following relationship: 'multiply a number by itself, add two then halve'. They decide to represent the relationship algebraically. They came up with the following solutions:

Zoe: $\dfrac{n \times n + 2}{2}$

David: $\dfrac{1}{2}\left(n^2 + 2\right)$

Zoe argues that their answers are different yet they both insist they are correct. What does this tell you about their understanding of algebraic expressions?

It is clear that David has a more sophisticated understanding of representing and manipulating algebraic expressions. Zoe has expressed the general relationship algebraically but, as yet, is unable to manipulate the expression in order to simplify it. What knowledge do you need to be able to effectively support and extend the development of their understanding of forming and manipulating algebraic expressions?

Simplifying algebraic expressions

In order to simplify algebraic expressions it is necessary to gather together or combine terms and powers wherever possible.

Terms are algebraic quantities that are separated from each other in expressions by + or − signs, e.g.:

Terms

Like terms are multiples of the same algebraic quantity. Hence, if terms are not of the same algebraic quantity they are **unlike** terms. For example:

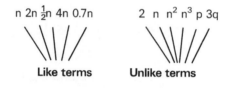

Like terms   Unlike terms

Hence, in order to simplify $(4n)^2 + 3n − 2 + 4n^2 − n + 7$ it is necessary first to identify like terms, then to combine them. It is often easier to group the like terms together within the expression then combine them:

$(4n)^2 + 3n − 2 + 4n^2 − n + 7$

$(4n × 4n) + 3n − 2 + 4n^2 − n + 7$

$16n^2 + 3n − 2 + 4n^2 − n + 7$

$16n^2 + 4n^2 + 3n − n − 2 + 7$

$20n^2 + 2n + 5$

Another useful strategy when simplifying expressions is to find factors. When considering numbers, any whole number that divides a given number exactly is called a factor of that number. This can be extended into the consideration of algebraic terms.

To find the factors of $4ab$ it is necessary to find all the terms which divide $4ab$ exactly, i.e.:

1, 2, 4, a, b, 2a, 2b, 4a, 4b, ab, 2ab, 4ab

PRACTICAL TASK

Use what you have discovered already to consider how the following might be simplified:

$8a^2 - ab + 4a^2 + 5ab$

Read on for further support.

First group like terms within the expression:

$8a^2 + 4a^2 - ab + 5ab$

Next combine like terms:

$12a^2 + 4ab$

Next identify a factor common to both the terms. The factor chosen is normally the highest common factor. 4a will divide exactly into $12a^2$ and $4ab$ (it is also the highest common factor of the terms) giving:

$4a (3a + b)$

Generally, to simplify expressions, combine terms and find factors.

General statements

Malik is asked to describe the sets of numbers that would be generated by the general statements 2n and 2n – 1.

The following answers were given:

2n represents the set of square numbers.

2n – 1 represents the set of square numbers minus one.

Is he correct? What sequences are represented by 2n and 2n – 1 ?

2n generates the following sequence of numbers:

2, 4, 6, 8, 10, ...

So it generates the set of even numbers.

2n – 1 generates the following sequence of numbers:

1, 3, 5, 7, 9, ...

So it generates the set of odd numbers.

What does this tell you about Malik's ability to interpret these general statements?

It is clear that he has misinterpreted the meaning of 2n in both cases. The answers clearly indicate a belief that it represents n x n or n^2. What knowledge do you need to be able to effectively support and develop his understanding of general statements?

Using algebra to describe sequences

It is possible to describe sequences briefly using algebra. The following sequence:

3,   6,   9,   12,   15,   ...

can be expressed as a general statement for multiples of three. To do this it is necessary to give each term a position in the sequence and find a relationship between the position and the term. In this case:

position: 1   2   3   4   5   ....   n

term: 3   6   9   12   15   ....   ?

To find the *nth* term it is necessary to look at the previous terms. It can clearly be seen that each term is equal to 3 multiplied by the position of the term. So the *nth* term here is 3 multiplied by *n* or 3*n*.

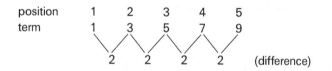

There are some rules which can be applied consistently when trying to establish general terms. Firstly look at the difference between the terms. This can give a big clue to help identify the general term, e.g.:

The fact that the difference is always 2 means that the general term will involve multiplication by 2. The only thing left to decide is, having multiplied the position by 2, what else needs to take place in order to arrive at the correct value for the term. In the above case it can be seen that, having multiplied by 2, 1 is then subtracted, giving 2n – 1.

Does this hold true for sequences with other differences? Yes, it does.

PRACTICAL TASK

Look at the following sequences. Try to work out their general terms.

position	1	2	3	4	5
term	1	4	7	10	13

position	1	2	3	4	5
term	5	9	13	17	21

Taking the first example, it can be seen that the difference between the terms is always 3. This indicates that the general case will involve multiplication by 3. What else is being done to the position number to achieve the term? Here 2 is being subtracted. This means the general term is 3n - 2.

In the second example, the difference is always 4, indicating that the position number will be multiplied by 4. Having multiplied by 4, 1 is then added, giving a general statement of 4n + 1.

This leads to a general case for all linear sequences which have a common difference (d):

$$a^n = dn + c$$

where a^n is the general term, d is the common difference and c is a constant.

But differences are not always the same. What can be established about a sequence if the difference between the terms is not the same?

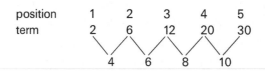

By looking at this it can be seen that the difference in each case is not the same. However, the difference in the differences is the same.

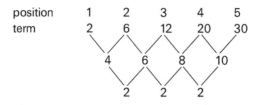

This fact indicates that the general statement is quadratic, i.e. it will contain a value for n multiplied by itself, i.e. n^2. Applying this to the above example, it is clear that the position is squared and then the position number is added to that answer, giving a general term $n^2 + n$. This can be neatly expressed as $n(n + 1)$.

This argument can be extended for greater powers of n.

Sequences – extension (for those who are interested)

The above explanation can be extended to offer a fuller description of this method. The method uses equivalent numerical and algebraic expressions.

Consider the following sequence:

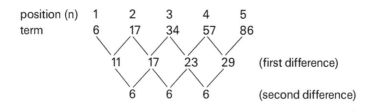

The fact that the sequence has a common second difference indicates that it is a quadratic, i.e. contains n^2. The general form of a quadratic expression is:

$an^2 + bn + c$ (where a, b, and c are constants)

Substituting n = 1, 2, 3, 4, 5 into the general expression gives:

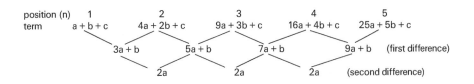

These two sequences and their differences are equivalent; one is the general case of the other.

By looking at the second differences it can be seen that 2a = 6, so a = 3.

Substitution can now be used to calculate values for b and c. Looking at the first differences and taking the difference between the n = 1 and n = 2 terms, it can be seen that 3a + b = 11. Substituting a = 3 gives b = 2.

Finally, looking at the first terms, it can be seen that a + b + c = 6. Substituting a = 3 and b = 2 gives c = 1.

Hence, the general or nth term is:

$$3n^2 + 2n + 1$$

This can be extended for other powers of n, e.g. a cubic expression has the general form $an^3 + bn^2 + cn + d$. This substitution method can be used here equally effectively.

Using algebra to prove general statements

This method of proof is included here as it demonstrates a useful aspect of algebra. There is plenty more about lots of different methods of proof in Chapter 4.

In mathematics it is possible to use summing to prove general statements and also **conjectures**. A conjecture is a hypothesis, something that has been surmised or deduced.

For more information on understanding equality, see Chapter 3.

One such instance is stating that adding consecutive odd numbers, starting at 1, will result in the square numbers, i.e.:

$$
\begin{aligned}
1 &= 1 &&= 1^2 \\
1 + 3 &= 4 &&= 2^2 \\
1 + 3 + 5 &= 9 &&= 3^2 \\
1 + 3 + 5 + 7 &= 16 &&= 4^2
\end{aligned}
$$

In order to prove this, it is necessary first to construct the general sequence of odd numbers (use the difference method above if necessary):

position	1	2	3	...	$(n-2)$	$(n-1)$	n
term	1	3	5	...	$(2n-5)$	$(2n-3)$	$(2n-1)$

If the sum of the first n odd numbers is S, then:

$$S = 1 + 3 + 5 + ... + (2n{-}5) + (2n{-}3) + (2n{-}1)$$

The expression that is equal to S can be written in reverse order without changing the value due to the commutative nature of addition:

$$S = (2n{-}1) + (2n{-}3) + (2n{-}5) + ... + 5 + 3 + 1$$

If these two values for S are added together a value for 2S is achieved:

$$2S = (1 + (2n - 1)) + (3 + (2n - 3)) + (5 + (2n - 5)) + ... + ((2n{-}5) + 5) + ((2n{-}3){+}3) + (2n{-}1) + 1)$$

$$2S = 2n + 2n + 2n + ... + 2n + 2n + 2n$$

$$2S = n \times 2n$$

$$2S = 2n^2$$

$$S = n^2$$

This shows that the sum of consecutive odd numbers, starting at 1, will result in a square number being generated.

Linear and simultaneous linear equations

RESEARCH SUMMARY

Lisa, in Year 6, is asked the following extension question:

If I go into a shop and buy two footballs and one tennis ball the cost is £3.00. If I buy one football and three tennis balls the cost is £2.75. How much do the football and tennis ball cost individually?

She decides the following: football – £1

tennis ball – £1

What does this tell you about her understanding of this problem?

It is clear that Lisa has not understood that both equations are required in order to solve this problem. She has merely selected numbers that would fit the first equation without using the second equation to inform her answer. What subject knowledge would you require to be able to extend Lisa's understanding?

An **equation** is a statement that two **expressions** are equal, e.g. $y = x + 2$. An **expression** is a general term used to describe mathematical terms, e.g. x^2. A **linear equation** takes the form:

$$ay + bx + c = 0$$

In the example $y = x + 2$, what are the values for a, b and c?

To work this out, it is necessary to rearrange the equation:

$$y = x + 2$$

$$y - x - 2 = 0$$

From this it is clear that a = 1, b = –1 and c = –2.

Because a linear equation does not involve any powers greater than 1, it can always be represented as a straight line graph. Equations involving greater powers of x are curves.

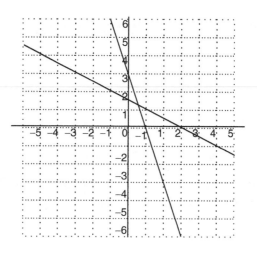

For more information on representing linear equations, see the section on graphs later in this chapter.

Lisa was attempting to solve **simultaneous linear equations**. Simultaneous linear equations are two linear equations which have a common solution. This means that for both equations, one value for *x* and the corresponding value for *y*, is common to them both. If the two equations were drawn on a graph, the lines would cross at the point where the values for the two equations were the same.

But how else can this problem be solved?

There are various ways of solving simultaneous linear equations. The first point to remember, and the point forgotten by Lisa, is that both equations are needed to find the solution.

Lisa attempted to 'guess' the answer. This is a valid method but requires the two equations in order to check the accuracy of the 'guess'. Once a 'guess' has been made, the next attempt can be refined in light of the outcome, gradually getting nearer and nearer until the answer is found. This method of trying an answer and learning something which is then applied to the next attempt can be described as **'trial and improvement'** (sometimes referred to as 'guess and check'). These are much more positive expressions than 'trial and error', which implies a mistake. Our phrases imply that learning is taking place in light of previous attempts. How might Lisa use trial and improvement to solve the problem?

two footballs and one tennis ball cost £3.00

one football and three tennis balls cost £2.75

Let the cost of the football be a pounds and the cost of the tennis ball b pounds.

The above equations can now be rewritten as

$2a + b = 3.00$

$a + 3b = 2.75$

Lisa's pattern of guesses might look something like this:

a	b	2a + b	a + 3b
1.00	1.00	3.00	4.00
1.15	0.70	3.00	3.25
1.25	0.50	3.00	2.75

So the prices are £1.25 for a football and 50p for a tennis ball.

There are other ways that you might choose to solve simultaneous equations yourself. One of these involves eliminating one of the unknowns. To do this it is necessary to multiply one of the equations to ensure there is an equal number of a particular unknown in both equations.

Let these two equations be called equation (1) and equation (2), i.e.

$2a + b = 3.00$ (1)

$a + 3b = 2.75$ (2)

If equation (1) is multiplied by 3 then both equations will have $3b$:

$6a + 3b = 9.00$ (1) ×3

If equation (2) is now subtracted from this new equation, the unknown $3b$ will be eliminated:

$$6a + 3b = 9.00$$
$$a + 3b = 2.75$$
$$5a \quad\;\; = 6.25$$
$$a \quad\;\; = 1.25$$

If the value for a is substituted back into equation (1) it will be possible to calculate the value for b:

$$2a + b = 3.00 \qquad (1)$$

$$2.50 + b = 3.00$$

$$b = 0.50$$

Hence, the football costs £1.25 and the tennis ball costs 50p.

Substituting a value in an equation, as in the final step above, can be used at the outset. This next method uses one of the equations to express one unknown in terms of the other unknown. This new expression is then substituted in the other equation, which is rearranged to find a solution, e.g.:

$$2a + b = 3.00 \qquad (1)$$

$$a + 3b = 2.75 \qquad (2)$$

Rearranging equation (2) gives:

$$a = 2.75 - 3b$$

This value for a is now substituted back into equation (1):

$$2(2.75 - 3b) + b = 3.00$$

$$5.50 - 6b + b = 3.00$$

$$5b = 2.50$$

$$b = 0.50$$

Substituting this value for b back into equation (2) gives:

$$a + 3b = 2.75$$

$$a + 1.50 = 2.75$$

$$a = 1.25$$

So the football costs £1.25 and the tennis ball costs 50p.

Functions and mappings

Luke is asked to identify the function in this problem:

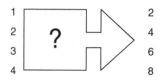

He decides that consecutive numbers are being added to themselves. What does this tell you about his understanding of expressing functions?

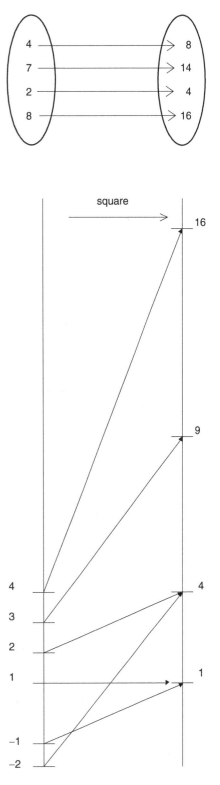

First, it can be seen that Luke has expressed in words the effect of multiplying consecutive numbers by two. However, he failed to express this as a functional relationship. What knowledge do you need to be able to effectively support and extend Luke's understanding of functions?

A **function** is a rule which changes or **maps** one number on to another. Functions or **mappings** can be represented in a range of different ways. The example above shows one representation. This idea of a 'function machine' is often found in primary schools. The number 1 is the input. It is put into the machine which then acts upon it with a consistent rule, in this case x2, to give 2 as the output. 2 is input to have 4 as the output, 3 to output 6, and so on.

These relations can also be shown as two sets, e.g.:

The first set (input) is also known as the **domain**. The second set (output) is known as the **range**.

Many functional relationships have a one-to-one relation, i.e. each member of the domain corresponds to one member of the range. Other functional relationships have a many-to-one relation, as illustrated on the right.

It is important to remember that, whether one-to-one or many-to-one, each member of the domain only ever corresponds to one member of the range.

Almost all the graphs children draw in school will be graphs of linear functions, i.e. for each value of the x-axis there is only one value on the y-axis.

Functions can also be used to represent the relationships when shapes are transformed. When a shape is transformed, e.g. translated, rotated, reflected or enlarged, each point on the shape is mapped onto another point.

Functions can be written in a number of ways. They are often represented with the letters f and g. Taking the example (left) of 'squaring', this could be written:

f changes x into x^2

or

$y = x^2$

or

f: $x \rightarrow x^2$

or

$f(x) = x^2$

Both x and y are variables, but x is said to be the **independent variable** and y is the **dependent variable** because x can take any number, but the value of y depends on the value of x.

PRACTICAL TASK

Consider the following function:

$f(x) = 2x + 1$

What would be the values for $f(x)$ corresponding to:

$x = 1, \quad x = 150, \quad x = 5.4, \quad x = -3$

It can be seen from the function that x first needs to be multiplied by 2 to give $2x$, in order to calculate the different values for $f(x)$. Having done that, 1 is added to achieve the $f(x)$ value. So:

$$x = 1 \qquad f(x) = (2 \times 1) + 1 = 3$$
$$x = 150 \qquad f(x) = (2 \times 150) + 1 = 301$$
$$x = 5.4 \qquad f(x) = (2 \times 5.4) + 1 = 11.8$$
$$x = -3 \qquad f(x) = (2 \times -3) + 1 = -5$$

Inverse functions

If it costs a school £200 per day for every supply teacher booked, it can clearly be seen that if the school uses 8 supply days in a term it will cost £1600. To work out the supply bill, the cost per day is multiplied by the number of days. Suppose the total supply bill is known: to calculate the number of supply days used, the total bill would need to be divided by the cost per day, i.e. $1600 \div 200 = 8$ This rule for 'undoing' the original function is called the **inverse function**. The inverse function is often represented as $f^{-1}(x)$.

If this 'undoing' rule is applied to the function from the example above, i.e. $f(x) = 2x + 1$, it is possible to calculate the inverse function.

From this it can be seen that the inverse function is:

$$f^{-1}(x) = \frac{x-1}{2}$$

What is the relationship between a function and its inverse?

The function $f(x)$ links the number x to the number $f(x)$. The inverse function $f^{-1}(x)$ links $f(x)$ back to x. This can be written as:

$$f^{-1}(f(x)) = x \text{ or } f(f^{-1}(x)) = x$$

This can be used to work out inverse functions when finding them by inspection is not easy.

Consider the example $f(x) = 2x + 1$. f

$(f^{-1}(x)) = x$ can be used to find the inverse function as follows:

$$f\left(f^{-1}(x)\right) = x$$
$$2\left(f^{-1}(x)\right) + 1 = x$$

$$2\left(f^{-1}(x)\right) = x - 1$$
$$f^{-1}(x) = \frac{x-1}{2}$$

Points to remember about finding inverse functions are that:

• only one-to-one functions have a unique inverse;
• the domain of the function is the range of the inverse and the range of the function is the domain of the inverse.

Graphs

A group of children is investigating circles. From practical activity they have recorded the diameters and circumferences for a range of circles. They use graphing software to produce the following graph:

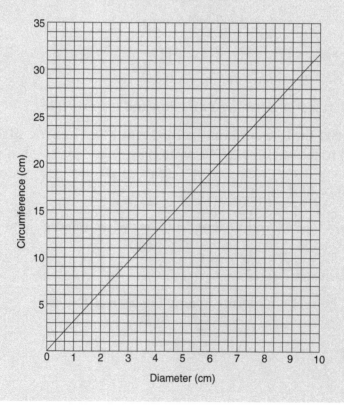

Laura is asked to use the graph to determine the circumference for circles with the following diameters:

(a) 3 cm   (b) 5 cm   (c) 8 cm

She decides the circumferences are:

(a) 10 cm   (b) 15 cm   (c) 25 cm

What does this tell you about her ability to interpret the information represented on the graph?

It can be seen that Laura has simply read the nearest labelled point on the vertical axis and therefore not understood that every point has a meaning. What subject knowledge do you need to be able to extend her understanding of interpreting graphical representation?

As stated earlier in this chapter, because a linear equation does not involve any powers greater than 1, it can always be represented as a straight line graph. Equations involving greater powers of x are curves.

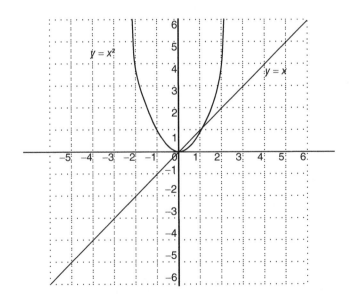

For more information on equations, look back earlier in this chapter to the section on linear and simultaneous equations.

As can be seen from the graph, $y = x$ is a straight line, i.e. **linear**, while $y = x^2$ (a **quadratic** equation) is a curve, in this case a parabola.

But given an equation, how are graphs drawn? And equally, given a graph, how is the equation determined?

Given any linear equation, it is possible to find points which will lie on the line. Taking the equation $y = 3x$, it can be seen that the points $(-2, -6)$, $(0, 0)$, $(1, 3)$, $(1.5, 4.5)$ will all lie on the line. The minimum number of points needed is three – this allows for a check point.

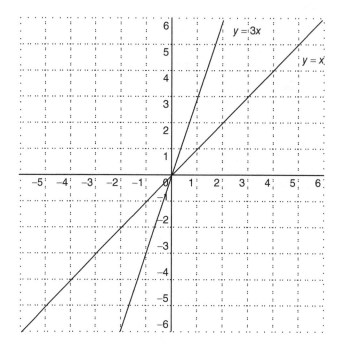

Compare this graph to the graph of $y = x$. It can be seen that they are both straight lines. However they have a different slope or **gradient**.

Gradient of a straight line

To calculate the gradient of a straight line (often called m), it is necessary to know the co–ordinates of two points. Taking $y = 3x$, the points $(-2, -6)$ and $(1, 3)$ lie on the line. To calculate the gradient the differences must be found

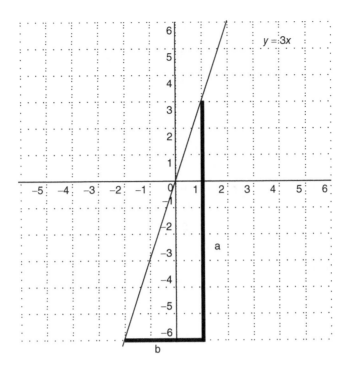

between the y co-ordinates (a) and the x co-ordinates (b), then the difference in the y co-ordinates is divided by the difference in the x co-ordinates, i.e. a ÷ b.

$$Gradient\,(m) = \frac{a}{b} = \frac{(3--6)}{(1--2)} = \frac{9}{3} = 3$$

It should be noted at this point that this value is equal to the value that x was multiplied by in the original equation, i.e. $y = 3x$.

So far this chapter has just considered graphs that pass through the origin, i.e. the point (0,0) lies on the graph. But what if a graph does not pass through the origin?

The y-intercept

Consider the graph of the linear function $y = x + 2$.

Straightaway it can be seen that the equation of this line differs from those encountered above (i.e. $y = x$ and $y = 3x$). This graph has the equation $y = x + 2$, i.e. something has been added. By looking at the graph of the equation it can

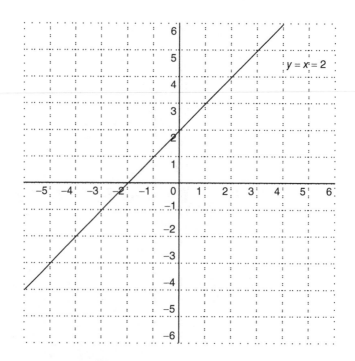

be seen that the graph crosses the y-axis at the point (0, 2), i.e. when $y = 2$, also known as the y-intercept. This is also the value of the number added to the x term in the equation. This number added to the x term is frequently called c.

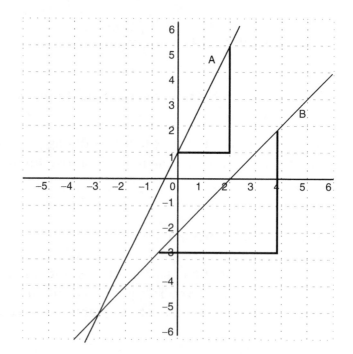

Finding equations of graphs

From the above it can be seen that it is possible to find the equation of a graph by calculating the gradient and finding the y-intercept. A linear equation has the general formula:

$$y = mx + c$$

where m is the gradient of the line and c is the y-intercept.

How could the equations of the lines on p. 130 be found?

Graph A:

Gradient (m) = 4 ÷ 2 = 2

y-intercept (c) = 1

Substituting these values into the general equation $y = mx + c$ gives:

$$y = 2x + 1$$

Graph B:

Gradient (m) = 5 ÷ 5 = 1

y-intercept (c) = –2

Substituting these values into the general equation $y = mx + c$ gives:

$$y = x - 2$$

Equally it is possible to identify the gradient and y-intercept of a graph from the equation of the line, e.g.:

$y = 4x + 3$ has a gradient of 4 and crosses the y-axis at the point (0, 3);

$2y = 6x + 1$ has a gradient of 3 (i.e. 6 ÷ 2) and y-intercept of $\frac{1}{2}$ (i.e. 1 ÷ 2)

But what happens if the equation is not written in the form $y = mx + c$?

To find the gradient and y-intercept if the equation is not of the form $y = mx + c$ involves rearranging the equation, e.g.:

$$x - 3y = 6$$
$$x = 6 + 3y$$
$$x - 6 = 3y$$

$$3y = x - 6$$
$$y = \frac{x}{3} - 2$$

So, the gradient is $\frac{1}{3}$ and the y-intercept is -2.

A SUMMARY OF KEY POINTS

- *Terms* are algebraic quantities that are separated from each other in expressions by + or –.
- General *terms* can be used to describe sequences.
- An *equation* is a statement that two expressions are equal.
- *Simultaneous linear equations* are two linear equations that have a common solution.
- There is a wide range of methods for solving simultaneous linear equations, including graphing, 'trial and improvement', eliminating unknowns and substitution.
- *Functions* are rules which change, or *map* one number onto another.
- Given a linear equation it is possible to establish the gradient and **y**-intercept of the graph it represents.

M-LEVEL EXTENSION

Think about the mathematical language that children will need to understand and use as they learn about algebra, equations, functions and graphs. At what ages/stages do aspects of this vocabulary become appropriate? You will find the suggested Further Reading section helpful in your reflections.

FURTHER READING

DfE (2011) *Teachers' Standards*. Available at https://www.gov.uk/government/uploads/system/uploads/attachment_data/file/301107/Teachers__Standards.pdf

Haylock, D. (2014) *Mathematics Explained for Primary Teachers*, 5th edn. London: Sage. As the title suggests, this book explains much of the content of the primary mathematics curriculum. It also addresses key teaching points and gives opportunities to try some self-assessment questions in each area, to further support your subject knowledge development.

Haylock, D. and Cockburn, A. (2017) *Understanding Mathematics for Young Children: A Guide for Teachers of Children 3–7*, 5th edn. London: Sage. This book aims to provide readers with a clearer understanding of the mathematics they will encounter in the classroom. Its focuses include mathematical symbolism and developing appropriate mathematical language.

https://study.sagepub.com/content/subject-knowledge-test-maths

An online self-audit to help identify areas of strength and further targets for development.

http://www.bbc.co.uk/schools/gcsebitesize/maths/

A useful site that, as the name suggests, breaks mathematics into 'bite-sized' pieces.

6
Measures

Teachers' Standards

A teacher must:

3. Demonstrate good subject and curriculum knowledge

    - have a secure knowledge of the relevant subject(s) and curriculum areas, foster and maintain pupils' interest in the subject, and address misunderstandings
    - demonstrate a critical understanding of developments in the subject and curriculum areas, and promote the value of scholarship

4. Plan and teach well structured lessons

    - impart knowledge and develop understanding through effective use of lesson time
    - promote a love of learning and children's intellectual curiosity
    - contribute to the design and provision of an engaging curriculum within the relevant subject area(s)

8. Fulfil wider professional responsibilities

    - take responsibility for improving teaching through appropriate professional development

Curriculum context

Early Years Foundation Stage

The Early Years Foundation Stage areas of learning and development recognise the importance of certain key skills in mathematical development, including 'measures'. By the end of the Foundation Stage most children will be able to use language such as 'more' or 'less', 'greater' or 'smaller' and 'heavier' or 'lighter' to compare two numbers or quantities, and use developing mathematical ideas and methods to solve practical problems.

National Curriculum programmes of study

At Key Stage 1, children use a range of measures to describe and compare different quantities such as length, mass, capacity/volume, time and money. During Lower Key Stage 2, children use measuring instruments with accuracy and make connections between measure and number.

During Upper Key Stage 2, during measurement children consolidate and extend their knowledge developed in number.

Measures

Introduction

Measurements are used throughout the world by people wishing to determine the physical features of an object such as its length or mass, or to chart the passing of time. However, the units of measure you encounter may not be the same the world over and even the quantity ascribed to certain measures differs. For example, in North America a pint has 16 fluid ounces, whereas a UK pint has 20 fluid ounces. This therefore means a US gallon is also proportionally smaller.

When children wish to measure they must first have acquired the language needed to describe the experience. Through discussion with peers, teachers and parents, they will have been exposed to the use of appropriate language for measures such as longer, shorter, heavier and wider. Children will have compared sizes such as pieces of birthday cake, bags of sweets and towers of bricks without having had the need to count. They will have used intuition and estimation skills for measuring before using arbitrary units such as shells and conkers. The understanding of the use of non-standard units such as cubes and cotton reels will have followed and finally the realisation that standard units such as metres, centimetres and kilograms are necessary in everyday life where the relationship of one measure to another is what is important.

This chapter discusses the stages of development in children's understanding of measures. It covers topics on the measurements of mass/weight, volume/capacity, time, length and surface area, and includes practical activities to help you to experience the concepts first-hand.

The stages of development in understanding measures

The following three stages are important in the teaching and learning of measures. It is important for your own subject knowledge that you understand the various stages and the associated vocabulary. The activities suggested here are merely examples to aid your understanding of the concept, although they can be used effectively in school.

Direct comparison using matching, with no actual measuring

Practical activities such as comparing the size of daddy bear's and mummy bear's bowls, the length of different children's hair or the weight of a bottle and a carton of juice are important at this stage for encouraging the development of language and mathematical vocabulary.

In addition to developing this measurement sense by comparing two lengths and asking questions such as 'how much longer?', we are introducing the concept of difference which will lead to a better understanding of subtraction later on. In addition, by introducing the idea of 'how many times as long?', we are paving the way to a better understanding of ratio and division.

Using non-standard units

In practical activities, children will use non-standard units such as shells, cupfuls, pebbles, beans, conkers, cubes and bricks. They need lots of experience with real-life objects and measuring length, area, volume, capacity and mass before they can begin to understand the concept of **conservation**. For example, if a piece of paper is torn in two or three pieces, does the surface area remain the same? If I break a ball of modelling clay into three smaller balls, do I still have the same weight of clay?

Using standard units

Having had experience in using non-standard units, children will begin to see the need for standard units. They will realise that by using non-standard units to compare the lengths, weights and capacities of objects their results may be unreliable and inconsistent. It is important that the skill of **estimation** is developed at this stage and that children should always be encouraged to offer an estimate before carrying out an activity. Your classroom should be a supportive environment where children are encouraged to take risks without fear of ridicule if they provide a 'wrong' answer. Children who are freed from the fear of criticism will more readily experiment with ideas and mathematical language. Estimating before a practical activity helps to dispel the belief that some children may have of mathematics; 'it is either right or wrong'. What is fundamentally important is that the process is more important than the product at this stage. A useful resource, which helps reinforce this skill, is an 'estimating table'. This could be an area of the classroom which has a small selection of everyday items on it such as a medium-sized apple, a packet of biscuits, a carton of fruit juice and a bag of sugar. Children could hold these items using their hand as a balance and write down their estimate of weight before posting it in a box on the display. At a certain time during the week, the teacher could open the box and read out the estimates before weighing the items and discussing the outcomes. This also has the benefit of helping the children to remember certain weights, and so when faced with an item whose weight they are unsure of, they can compare it with an item already known. For example 'I know that a bag of sugar weighs 1 kg/2.2 lb, so I can use that knowledge to work out the weight of another item I am unsure of'.

RESEARCH SUMMARY

Having considered this three-stage development of direct comparison, non-standard units and standard units, it is interesting to review some of the other research that has been conducted in the area of children developing measurement concepts. Clements and Stephan (2003) summarised some interesting contradictions. The three-stage process advocated in England and in many other places is firmly based in Piaget's developmental theory of measurement. The argument is that this approach enables students to see the need for a standard unit.

However, Clements and Stephan also summarised the work of other researchers, including Clements et al. (1997), Boulton-Lewis et al. (1996) and Nunes et al. (1993), whose conclusions questioned the wisdom of first concentrating on non-standard units. They found that young children were unsuccessful when using non-standard units; however, they found that they could be successful at an earlier age with standard units and measuring instruments. Clements and Stephan concluded that these outcomes support a Vygotskian perspective, with rulers viewed as cultural instruments which children can appropriate.

What is certain is that measurement forms an integral part of our daily lives and children need to be enabled to develop 'measurement sense' successfully.

Understanding units and measures

The standard units of measures you'll need to know are set out below, followed by *approximate* equivalences:

	Metric	Imperial
Weight (Mass)	g, kg, tonnes	ounces, pounds, stones
Volume	cm³, m³	cubic inches/feet
Capacity	ml, cl, litre	fluid ounces, pints, gallons
Length	cm, m, km	inches, feet, yards, miles
Area	cm², m², hectares	square inches/feet/yards
Time		seconds, minutes, hours

	Metric	Imperial
Weight (Mass)	28 g	1 oz
	1 kg	2.2 1b
	50 kg	8 stones
	1 tonne	1 ton
Volume	16 cm³	1 cubic inch
	1 m³	35 cubic feet
Capacity	570 ml	1 pint
	1 litre	1.75 pints
	4.5 litres	1 gallon
Length	2.5 cm	1 inch
	30 cm	1 foot
	1 m	39 inches
	8 km	5 miles
Area	6.5 cm²	1 square inch
	1 m²	11 square feet

Although in Britain today we still refer to **imperial measures** (introduced in the Magna Carta in 1215), such as pints, gallons and miles, on a daily basis, the metric system is widely recognised as being the most commonly used system for measuring. Indeed, since 2000, the metric system has had to take precedence over the imperial system in retailing. Unlike the imperial system where differences can exist in exactly what quantity a word is specifying (see 'pint' in the introduction to this chapter), the metric system is the same wherever it is used. The **Système International**, or **S.I.**, determines the units of measurement used in the metric system. They include:

- millimetres, centimetres, metres, kilometres – length, area;
- grams, kilograms – mass;
- seconds, minutes, hours – time;
- millilitres, litres – capacity;
- cubic centimetres – volume;
- degrees – angles.

Mass and weight

REFLECTIVE TASK

Akeva weighs a ball of modelling clay and says it weighs 150 g. He then breaks up the ball into a number of pieces and says it will weigh more because there are more pieces. What subject knowledge do you need to effectively support and develop Akeva's understanding of mass and weight?

To begin with, it is necessary for you to understand the difference between mass and weight. These terms are commonly used as if they are interchangeable. In fact, mass is the amount of matter in an object and it is measured in grams and kilograms. When faced with the concept of mass, the problem we have is that we cannot directly see or feel the amount of matter in an object. When we hold something in our hand, it is the force we are feeling which determines how heavy the object appears. It is this force which affects the weight of an object. Hence, weight is a measure of force, measured in newtons. Clearly the weight will change depending on how far you are from the centre of the Earth. We know that when the gravitational pull of astronauts in space is less than on the Earth, then they experience weightlessness – clearly their mass has not changed.

Children come to school with a wide experience of mass and weight. For example, they have weighed out ingredients for baking a cake; they have heard discussions at home about dieting and losing 'weight'; they have seen vegetables and fruit being weighed in the supermarket, and cheese and ham being weighed in the deli and therefore, understandably, find difficulty when faced with a new word which deals with the concept of weight as they know it. When weighing an amount of cheese we say it is 250 grams. What we mean is that its weight is equal to a 250-gram mass and that its mass is 250 grams. If we wish to lose weight ourselves then it's a trip to the moon we need! We can weigh 60 kg on our bathroom scales at home here on earth but were we to take these scales and weigh ourselves on the moon, we would find that we weighed a mere sixth of our weight on earth, just 10 kg! We do not lose weight when we diet; we lose some of our mass.

Because the concepts of mass and weight are used interchangeably socially, the National Curriculum decided that, in the early stages of learning, children will be taught about 'weight' even though, technically, the concept is 'mass'.

As children progress from Key Stage 2 to Key Stage 3 the concepts of mass and weight can be explored in greater depth. One outcome is, as a society, we will probably continue to use the two words as if they are synonymous. As a teacher, simply make sure you know the difference between mass and weight and can explain it to children if and when you need to.

Volume and capacity

REFLECTIVE TASK

Having filled a saucepan with water and then placed a number of large potatoes in it, Joe notices that the water begins to overflow. He suggests that if he chops up the potatoes into smaller pieces the water will not rise as much. What knowledge do you need in order to move Joe's learning on?

According to Archimedes' principle, a body partially or wholly submerged in liquid experiences an upward force equal to the weight of fluid it displaces.

As with mass and weight, it is important that the distinction between the meaning of **volume** and the meaning of **capacity** is made. When we talk about volume we mean the amount of three-dimensional space something occupies and we normally measure this in cubic units. Capacity, on the other hand, refers to the actual container and describes how much liquid volume it can hold when full. Capacity is measured in millilitres or litres. In primary schools you will focus on the teaching of capacity; however, we shall also address volume here to ensure you are confident about both concepts.

PRACTICAL TASK

How many differently shaped boxes with a volume of 20 cubic centimetres can you make?

Archimedes told us how to find the volume of our hand by placing it in a container full of water and measuring the amount of water that has been displaced by it. Pour the amount of displaced water into a measuring jug and then convert the amount of millilitres you have displaced into cubic centimetres.

Investigating Archimedes' principle of water displacement will further enhance your knowledge and understanding of the links between cubic centimetres and millilitres.

PRACTICAL TASK

Try placing a variety of irregularly shaped objects in a cylinder of water. Take note of the level of water in the cylinder before you start and watch how the water line is raised when you place the object in the cylinder. By how much did the level of the water rise? You can now find the difference between the original level of water in the cylinder and the higher level. Convert the millilitres to cubic centimetres and you will have found the volume of an irregular shape.

Finding volumes of regular shapes can be done by filling the shape with cubic centimetres. You will begin to notice that the number of cubic centimetres you need to cover the base will tell you the area of the base. Count how many cubic centimetres high your container is. If you multiply the area of the base of your container by its height your answer should be equivalent to the number of cubes you have in your container (see below). By carrying out these activities you are demonstrating the links between the measurement of volume and capacity.

The discovery that 1 litre of water has the same volume as 1000 cubic centimetres is a very important one. Through further investigation, children will also discover the relationship between millilitres, cubic centimetres and grams. The mass of 1 kilogram of water is equivalent to 1 litre or 1000 cubic centimetres.

- The volume of a cube/cuboid is given by length × breadth × height (l × b × h).

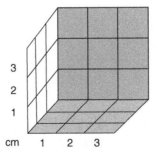

Figure 6.1 Finding the volume of a regular shape

For more information on polyhedra, see Chapter 7.

The volume of prisms

Having found the volume of cubes and cuboids by filling them with centimetre cubes, then by using the formula of area of base times height, we can now work out the volume of half a cube or cuboid. Knowing that making a diagonal cut through a cube yields two identical triangular prisms should help you to understand that each of these triangular prisms will have the volume of half the cube. The bases of the prisms are right-angled triangles, whose area will be half that of the square face of the cube. By multiplying the area of the base of the prism by its height we can find the volume of a triangular prism.

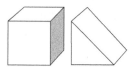

- The volume of a triangular prism is half (length x breadth x height) $\frac{1}{2}$ (l × b × h).

Cones and cylinders

> ## PRACTICAL TASK
>
> How can we find the volume of a cone? Is there a relationship between the volume of a cone and the volume of a cylinder?
>
> Make a cone and a cylinder out of card, making sure they are of equal height and have an equal radius. Now measure how much sand is needed to fill each one completely. Try repeating this with different pairs of cones and cylinders. Can you see a relationship between how much sand the cone holds and how much its 'partner' cylinder holds? By repeating this a number of times with different cones and cylinders you should begin to see a pattern in your results. Within the limits of experimental accuracy, you should discover that the volume of the cone is one third the volume of the cylinder.
>
> You could also refer to Archimedes' displacement principle again and immerse a cone and a cylinder of equal height and radius in containers of liquid and measure how much liquid is displaced - not recommended for use with cardboard shapes! You could try making them with modelling clay.

- The volume of a cylinder is given by πr²h (πr² being the area of the circular base).
- The volume of a cone is given by $\frac{1}{3}$πr²h (i.e. $\frac{1}{3}$ of the volume of the cylinder).

PRACTICAL TASK

Use three pieces of card which are equal in size. Make a cylinder, cuboid and triangular prism. Predict which container will have the greatest volume. Fill them with sand. Which holds the most sand? Why?

For more information on polyhedra, see Chapter 7.

Surface area

The surface area of a **polyhedron** is equal to the sum of the area of its faces. To calculate the surface area of a cube you simply need to know the length of one **edge** (L). From this it is possible to calculate the area of each face (L × L) and multiply it by the number of faces – in this case 6. This will give you the answer 6L². For a cuboid it is necessary to know the length, breadth and height in order to be able to calculate the area of each face and thus the overall surface area.

To calculate the surface area of a cylinder it is necessary to calculate the areas of the two circular faces and then to calculate the area of the curved face which, if rolled out, you will realise is actually a rectangle.

Remember:

- Area of a circle = πr².
- Circumference of a circle = 2πr

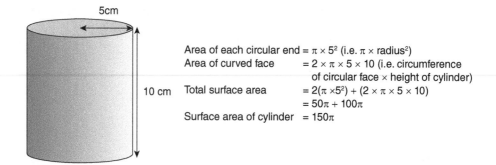

Area of each circular end $= \pi \times 5^2$ (i.e. $\pi \times$ radius^2)
Area of curved face $= 2 \times \pi \times 5 \times 10$ (i.e. circumference of circular face $\times$ height of cylinder)
Total surface area $= 2(\pi \times 5^2) + (2 \times \pi \times 5 \times 10)$
$= 50\pi + 100\pi$
Surface area of cylinder $= 150\pi$

Time

You ask one of your pupils, Julie, this question: if we leave for our holiday at 09:43 hours and arrive at our destination at 13:15 hours, how long did our journey take?

Julie answers 3 hours 72 minutes and shows you her method:

$$
\begin{array}{r}
13:15 \\
-09:43 \\
\hline
03:72
\end{array}
$$

Is Julie correct? What method has she used? Is it appropriate? From her working it can be seen that Julie has used a subtraction algorithm using a base-10 place value system. She has not recognised that this will not work with time calculations, which use 60 minutes to the hour and 24 hours to the day.

For more information on subtraction, see Chapter 2.

There are two aspects of time which children need to understand. Firstly there is the interval of time, for example the time between morning play and lunchtime; the time between my birthday and yours; the time between Easter and summer. These intervals are measured in seconds, minutes, days, weeks, months, years, decades, etc. Children use their memory and important events which provide landmarks to understand the passing of time. The second aspect of time is recorded time. This is the time that something happens. We use analogue or digital time and the date to say exactly when an event occurred. An example of this might be:

'The school concert will take place on Saturday 24 October 2012 at 7:30 p.m.'

If we were to state that the expected finishing time of the concert was 10 p.m., then we could work out the interval of time between the start and the finish as being two and a half hours. When calculating the time interval between two times, using a standard written algorithm is not recommended. The method known as 'shopkeeper's addition' or 'complementary addition' is the most useful way of calculating the difference between two times. Start with 7:30 and work out how many minutes till 8:00 (30). Now work out how many hours from 8:00 until 10:00 (2). Add your results together and you will get two and a half hours or two hours 30 minutes.

For further information on the use of language in mathematics, see Chapter 4.

The 24 hour clock

As this system is now used for rail, air, bus and boat timetables as well as video/DVD recorders, microwaves and watches, you will need to be familiar with it and its relationship with the 12 hour clock. In this system we always use four digits to express the time. We use the first two digits for the hours and the last two for the minutes. When we wish to say the time is 13:30, we say: 'The time is thirteen thirty'. It is important not to confuse the language here with the language of decimal notation, where 13.30 would be read as, 'thirteen point three'. Using a colon not a point when writing time in this way helps to reinforce this distinction.

A further source of confusion is use of 'fifteen hundred' which is used to express the time 15:00. It suggests that the presence of two zeros means a hundred, which is a common misunderstanding amongst children.

For more information on complementary addition, see Chapter 2.

Because time is non-metric, children need to learn that bridging through 10 or 100 is not always appropriate. A digital clock displaying 7:59 will in two minutes display 8:01, not 7:61. When working with minutes and hours it is necessary to bridge through 60, and with hours and days through 24. Digital clocks could suggest to children that minutes behave like 'ordinary' numbers and so they might count on 59, 60, 61, not realising that when 60 is reached they have reached a new hour and must go back to zero with their counting. It is important therefore that you plan activities and discussion around this potential misconception. Reference to the clock face should help children see why this form of counting is not appropriate under these circumstances.

PRACTICAL TASK

The ferry leaves the island at 09:43. It reaches the mainland at 13:15. How long is the journey from the island to the mainland?

To calculate the difference, start with 09:43 and count on to 10:00. How many minutes have you counted on? (17) From 10:00 to 13:00 it is another 3 hours. So far we have 3 hours and 17 minutes. From 13:00 hours to 13:15 is another 15 minutes. Added together we have 3 hours, 17 minutes and 15 minutes. This makes 3 hours 32 minutes altogether. Written as a standard algorithm this calculation would be cumbersome and open to misconceptions. It may look like this:

$$\begin{array}{r} {\scriptstyle 0\ 12\ \ 7} \\ 13:15 \\ -\ \ 9:43 \\ \hline 3:32 \end{array}$$

The abbreviations a.m. and p.m.

The abbreviation a.m. is for ante-meridiem, meaning before noon, and p.m. is an abbreviation for post-meridiem, meaning after noon. This means that 12 noon is neither a.m. nor p.m. and similarly that 12 midnight is neither a.m. nor p.m. We say 12 noon or 12 midnight when we wish to make the distinction between them. In the 24 hour system the time one minute after 23:59 is not 24:00 but 00:00, the beginning of a new day, and we call this 'zero hours'. However, when the time is zero hours it does not mean that time has disappeared. Likewise, when the thermometer reads zero degrees there is still a temperature that we can feel. This is the main distinction between a **ratio scale** and an **interval scale**.

In a ratio scale, the zero means nothing, e.g. a length of zero metres is no length, a mass of zero grams is nothing, and a bottle containing zero millilitres is empty.

Interval scales

Comparing two times gives us the difference in time between the two. It does not tell us that 2 o'clock is three times less than 6 o'clock. It tells us that 2 o'clock is 4 hours earlier than 6 o'clock. This is an example of an interval scale. Similarly when comparing two temperatures we cannot say, because it is 15 degrees here and 45 degrees elsewhere, it is three times hotter in the other place.

A SUMMARY OF KEY POINTS

- Estimation and approximation are fundamental to measuring.
- Discovery through practical work is essential for the understanding of measures, e.g. while working with shape and space, include calculating and measuring length, area, volume and capacity to underpin knowledge and understanding of compound measures.
- Acknowledge the incorrect use of 'weight' in daily use.
- Children need to understand the relationship between measures, e.g. cubic centimetres and millilitres, and know that 1 kg = 1l = 1000 cubic centimetres.

M-LEVEL EXTENSION

Look again at the Research Summary of the work of Clements and Stephan (2003). Some of the research that they reviewed seemed to contradict the three-stage model of the development of children's understanding of measurement. Find out more about the Vygotskian perspective, and talk to experienced colleagues about this issue. What is your view?

Transitive property is explained on page 61 in Chapter 3.

FURTHER READING

DfE (2011) *Teachers' Standards*. Available at https://www.gov.uk/government/uploads/system/uploads/attachment_data/file/301107/Teachers__Standards.pdf

Haylock, D. (2014) *Mathematics Explained for Primary Teachers*, 5th edn. London: Sage. This book is essential reading for primary teachers who wish to increase their confidence in mathematics. The chapter on measures clearly defines the principles which are central to teaching measurement in the primary school.

https://study.sagepub.com/content/subject-knowledge-test-maths

An online self-audit to help identify areas of strength and further targets for development.

http://www.bbc.co.uk/schools/gcsebitesize/maths/

A useful site that, as the name suggests, breaks mathematics into 'bite-sized' pieces.

7
Geometry

Teachers' Standards

A teacher must:

3. Demonstrate good subject and curriculum knowledge

    - have a secure knowledge of the relevant subject(s) and curriculum areas, foster and maintain pupils' interest in the subject, and address misunderstandings
    - demonstrate a critical understanding of developments in the subject and curriculum areas, and promote the value of scholarship

4. Plan and teach well structured lessons

    - impart knowledge and develop understanding through effective use of lesson time
    - promote a love of learning and children's intellectual curiosity
    - contribute to the design and provision of an engaging curriculum within the relevant subject area(s)

8. Fulfil wider professional responsibilities

    - take responsibility for improving teaching through appropriate professional development

Curriculum context

Early Years Foundation Stage

The Early Years Foundation Stage recognises the importance of certain key skills in mathematical development. The areas of learning identified include working with shape and space.

By the end of the Foundation Stage, children are expected to recognise, create and describe patterns. They explore characteristics of everyday objects and shapes and use mathematical language to describe them.

National Curriculum programmes of study

The Mathematics National Curriculum clearly states the knowledge, skills and understanding which are to be taught throughout the key stages.

At Key Stage 1, children will recognise and name common 2-D and 3-D shapes. They also describe position, direction and movement. At Lower Key Stage 2, children draw and make shapes and compare and classify shapes. They recognise angles, identify horizontal, vertical, perpendicular and parallel lines. They identify lines of symmetry.

At Upper Key Stage 2 children classify shapes with increasingly complex geometric properties and they learn the vocabulary they need to describe them.

Geometry

Introduction

An understanding of shape and space is vital to us as people who live in and move around a three-dimensional world. As we attempt to make sense of that world, we develop visual images and vocabulary to support our developing spatial understanding. We represent our 3-D environment within 2-D media, e.g. in pictures and text, and we use language to describe our position and movements. Understanding geometry is therefore crucial as we explore and extend our understanding of shape, space and movement.

This chapter looks at the systematic naming of 2-D and 3-D shapes, identifies their properties and considers transformation of 2-D shapes. It explains Pythagoras' theorem in respect of work on triangles, and the use of pi (π) in work on circles. Surface area and volume are considered in detail. Cartesian co-ordinates are introduced as a way of expressing where in space, in one and four quadrants, something is located, and angles are considered.

RESEARCH SUMMARY

Jones and Mooney (2003) discussed the status of geometry within primary schools. They recognised the importance of geometry within an increasingly technological society, with web graphics and computer-generated images being part of the everyday experience of many people. If schools are to deliver a relevant mathematics curriculum, then the importance of teaching geometry cannot be overemphasised.

Sir Michael Atiyah (2001) argued that along with algebra, geometry is one of the two pillars of mathematics. He believes that geometry is so fundamental to our experience of mathematics that we endeavour to put things into a geometrical form, as this enables us to use our intuition. This notion of using visual imagery is further supported by Whiteley (2004, page 1)

(Continued)

(Continued)

when he states, *It is an illusion that mathematical reasoning is done in the brain with language.* This is quite a provocative statement as it can be construed as presenting an opposite stance to that of current socio-cultural approaches in mathematics education, which encourage the regular use of communication, implying the need for appropriate mathematical language. However, it should not be viewed so simplistically as being that either children are encouraged to use mathematical language, or children are encouraged to use visualisation. The reality is a combination of the two. Whiteley (2004, page 3) goes on to describe visual reasoning as *seeing to think*. This really brings the two together. Visualisation is a power tool in all areas of mathematics, but particularly within geometry. Having the opportunity of *seeing to think* enables children to engage with the problem in a meaningful way; having access to appropriate mathematical language enables them to communicate this thinking to others.

Polygons

REFLECTIVE TASK

Alex's teacher asks him to name the following shapes and then identify the numbers of lines of reflective symmetry and the orders of **rotational symmetry**.

Shape 1   Shape 2

Alex decides the following:

- Shape 1 is an octagon. It has 16 lines of reflective symmetry and rotational symmetry of order 9.
- Shape 2 is a star. It has 8 lines of reflective symmetry and rotational symmetry of order 5.

What does this tell you about his understanding of polygons?

It is clear that Alex solely associates the polygon names with regular polygons and not with irregular ones. It is also evident that Alex is drawing lines of reflective symmetry and then counting both ends; not recognising them as lines that bisect the shape. When considering rotational symmetry Alex is counting the 'starting' position twice, once at the beginning and again when the final rotation is made.

What knowledge do you need to be able to effectively support and extend his understanding of naming polygons?

Naming polygons

'Polygon' comes from the Greek *poly* meaning 'many' and *gon* from *gonu* meaning 'knee', so a polygon is a shape with many knees!

It would be possible to keep naming polygons indefinitely and scholars have worked out systems to keep naming polygons up to those with millions of sides. However, within primary mathematics it is more usual to deal with polygons up to a dodecagon (12 sides):

3 sides: triangle (also sometimes referred to as a trigon for mathematical consistency)	6 sides: hexagon
	7 sides: heptagon
	8 sides: octagon
4 sides: quadrilateral (also sometimes referred to as a tetragon for mathematical consistency)	9 sides: enneagon (frequently referred to as a nonagon)
	10 sides: decagon
	11 sides: hendecagon
5 sides: pentagon	12 sides: dodecagon

If you are interested in finding out more about naming polygons with a greater number of sides there are plenty of websites containing this information. One easy to understand site is http://faculty.kutztown.edu/schaeffe/Tutorials/General/Polygons.html

Regular or irregular polygons?

From the responses it is clear that Alex did not understand the concept of regular and irregular polygons. If a polygon is regular this indicates that all its sides are of equal length and all the interior angles are the same size. If it is irregular then its sides are not of the same length, nor are its interior angles all the same size. Thus, the 'star' identified by Alex is an irregular octagon.

Reflective symmetry

Alex was not successful in identifying the number of lines of reflective symmetry. A shape is said to have reflective or line symmetry if you can fold it so that one half fits exactly on top of the other half. The line through the middle, the line of symmetry, is like a mirror; each half is a reflection of the other.

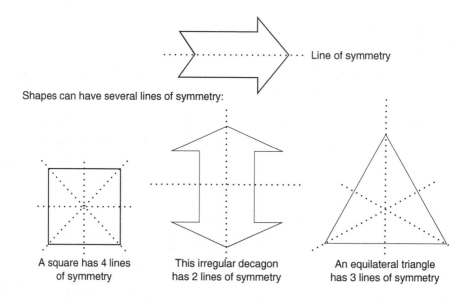

Line of symmetry

Shapes can have several lines of symmetry:

A square has 4 lines
of symmetry

This irregular decagon
has 2 lines of symmetry

An equilateral triangle
has 3 lines of symmetry

A regular polygon has the same number of lines of symmetry as the number of its sides. Alex correctly identified the lines of symmetry but counted them incorrectly. By counting around the octagon, he counted both ends of each line and thus counted every line twice, ending up with an answer twice that of the correct answer.

Rotational symmetry

Alex was not successful in identifying the orders of rotational symmetry. A shape is said to have rotational symmetry if it looks the same in different positions when rotated about its centre.

In Figure 7.1, the spot in each of the squares is to help with identifying the order of rotational symmetry and should not be considered as part of the square or the centre of rotation.

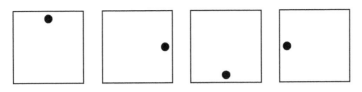

Figure 7.1 Rotational symmetry

It can be seen that, in each of the four positions above, the square looks exactly the same, so the order of rotational symmetry of the square is 4.

Try this with a rectangle (use a book or a piece of A4 paper) and you will notice that a rectangle has rotational symmetry of order 2.

What do you notice about regular polygons? A regular polygon has an order of rotational symmetry equal to the number of sides.

Any shape, however strange, will have rotational symmetry of order 1, since there is one position where it looks the same!

Alex understood that in order to identify the order of rotation it was necessary to rotate about a point. However, he then counted the starting position twice, once at the beginning and again at the end of the count. Therefore the answer in both cases was one greater than the correct order.

Triangles

Unlike many other polygons, different kinds of triangles have different names. Thus, it is possible to give specific names to irregular triangles based on their particular properties (see Figure 7.2).

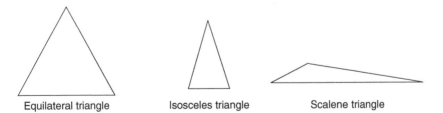

Equilateral triangle   Isosceles triangle   Scalene triangle

Figure 7.2 Different kinds of triangle

A regular triangle is called an **equilateral triangle**. Because it is a regular polygon it is clear that all the sides must be of equal length and all the interior angles must be the same size (60°). Again, because an equilateral triangle is regular, it must also have three lines of reflective symmetry and rotational symmetry of order 3.

A triangle which has two sides of equal length is called an **isosceles triangle**. As well as having two sides of equal length, an isosceles triangle also has two angles of equal size. An isosceles triangle has one line of reflective symmetry and rotational symmetry of order 1. The name 'isosceles' derives from the Greek *iso* (same) and *skelos* (leg).

A triangle which has three sides of different length and no equal angles is called a **scalene triangle**. Scalene triangles have no lines of reflective symmetry and rotational symmetry of order 1.

A triangle containing one angle of 90° is called a right-angled triangle. A right-angled triangle will also be either isosceles or scalene (see Figure 7.3).

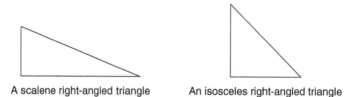

A scalene right-angled triangle   An isosceles right-angled triangle

Figure 7.3 Right-angled triangles

The number of lines of reflective symmetry of a right-angled triangle depends on whether it is isosceles or scalene. The right-angled triangle is also a special shape as it is possible to use Pythagoras' theorem to calculate the length of the longest side.

Pythagoras' theorem

Pythagoras (582–507 BCE) was a Greek philosopher and geometrician. He founded the Pythagorean Brotherhood, a secretive group who refused to share their mathematical discoveries. It all backfired in a rather unpleasant way when, owing to the suspicion and fear of the locals, and encouraged by a rival of Pythagoras, many of the Brotherhood, including their leader, were killed when their buildings were set alight.

Pythagoras' theorem states that it is possible to calculate the length of the longest side (the hypotenuse) of a right-angled triangle by finding the square root of the sum of the squares of the other two sides of the triangle. In some right-angled triangles it is very simple to work out the length of the hypotenuse because all the numbers work out as whole numbers. If a triangle has two sides, one of 3 cm and the other of 4 cm, what is the length of the hypotenuse?

$c = \sqrt{(9 + 16)}$

$c = \sqrt{25}$

$c = 5$

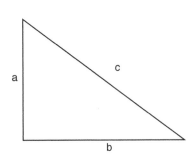

So the hypotenuse is 5 cm long.

This will also be true for multiples of these numbers, e.g.:

if a = 6 and b = 8 then c = 10 because 36 + 64 = 100

Another set of numbers which is easy to calculate is a = 5 and b = 12. What is the length of the hypotenuse here?

$c = \sqrt{(25 + 144)}$

$c = \sqrt{169}$

$c = 13$

So the hypotenuse is 13 cm long.

Sets of three whole numbers that perfectly fit Pythagoras' equation are called Pythagorean triples.

How does this work? The following diagrams show how Pythagoras' theorem works.

Taking the 3 cm, 4 cm, 5 cm right-angled triangle the following can be seen:

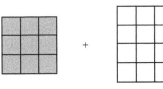 + 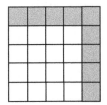 =

From this it is clear that $3^2 + 4^2 = 5^2$.

The following diagram illustrates how this can be shown, starting with any right-angled triangle:

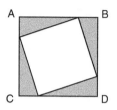

The square in the middle of the four triangles is the square on the hypotenuse of any of these triangles.

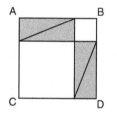

The square ABCD remains unchanged. By moving the four triangles it is possible to create two squares instead of one. These two squares are on the other two sides of the triangle. Because the area of ABCD remains unchanged the sum of the areas of the two smaller squares must be equal to the area of the square on the hypotenuse.

For more information on Pythagoras' theorem, see Chapter 4.

Quadrilaterals

Just as with triangles, irregular quadrilaterals can also be named. Again, the names depend on the properties of the particular quadrilateral (see Figure 7.4).

A regular quadrilateral is called a **square**. Because it is a regular polygon it is clear that all the sides must be of equal length and all the interior angles must be the same size (90°). The diagonals of a square are equal in length and bisect each other (i.e. cut each other in half) at right angles. Because a square is regular it must also have four lines of reflective symmetry and rotational symmetry of order 4.

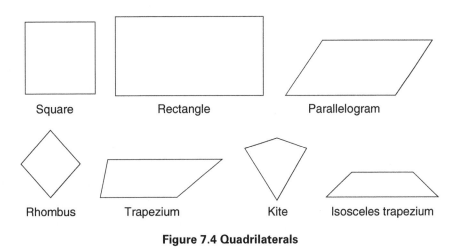

Figure 7.4 Quadrilaterals

A **rectangle** has four right angles, the opposite sides are of equal length and parallel. The diagonals are also equal in length and bisect each other. Rectangles have at least two lines of reflective symmetry and rotational symmetry of order 2. Why 'at least'? Because a square has all the characteristics required of a rectangle – it has four right angles, the opposite sides are equal in length and parallel and the diagonals are equal in length and bisect each other; thus, a square also falls into the rectangle category, but has four lines of symmetry and rotational symmetry of order 4, hence the 'at least'.

When is a rectangle not a square? When it is an **oblong**! An oblong is a 2-D shape that can be described as 'a rectangle which is not a square'.

A **parallelogram** has opposite sides that are equal in length and parallel and the opposite angles are of equal size. The diagonals bisect each other. Parallelograms have a rotational symmetry of at least order 2. Again it is 'at least' because there are some special cases which fit the description of a parallelogram but have different symmetry properties.

Are the square and the rectangle parallelograms?
Yes. They both have all the characteristics required of a parallelogram. They both have opposite sides which are equal in length and parallel, they have opposite angles which are equal and their diagonals bisect each other.

There is one further quadrilateral which is also a special case of parallelogram and that is the **rhombus**. A rhombus has four sides that are equal in length. Opposite sides are parallel and opposite angles are of equal size. The diagonals bisect each other at right angles. A rhombus has at least two lines of reflective symmetry and rotational symmetry of order 2. If the interior angles of the rhombus are equal (i.e. 90°) then it is also a square.

Another quadrilateral that has characteristics which can be satisfied by many of the other quadrilaterals above is the **trapezium**. Generally a trapezium has one pair of parallel sides. As can be seen from Figure 7.4, it does not need to have any other characteristics regarding symmetry properties, length of sides, size of angles or diagonals to be a trapezium. However, if a trapezium has 'legs' of equal length it is a special case of trapezium.

An **isosceles trapezium** has one pair of parallel sides; the other pair of sides is equal in length (remember 'same legs'?). It also has base angles which are the same size and diagonals which are equal in length. It has a line of reflective symmetry.

Looking at the definition of a trapezium it is clear that a square, a rectangle, a parallelogram and a rhombus could all be considered as a trapezium.

The final quadrilateral is the **kite**. This has two adjacent pairs of sides that are equal in length and at least one pair of opposite angles equal. The diagonals cross at right angles. A kite has at least one line of reflective symmetry. A rhombus and a square can also be considered a kite.

REFLECTIVE TASK

In a geoboard investigation the children are asked to find as many different triangles as possible. Kylie finds 12.

What does this tell you about Kylie's understanding of congruence, similarity and 2-D transformations?

Kylie does not yet understand the concept of congruence. What knowledge do you need to support your teaching to develop her understanding of congruence?

Congruence, 2-D transformations and similarity

Congruence

Shapes are said to be congruent if they are the same shape and size. The orientation and position of the shapes do not matter as they do not alter the shape itself.

PRACTICAL TASK

Look at the following triangles.

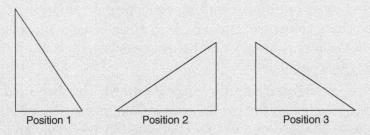

Position 1   Position 2   Position 3

Are they congruent? What transformations have taken place moving from position 1 to position 2 and position 3?

These triangles are congruent as they are the same shape and size. The orientation and position have altered but the shape and size remain unchanged. In order to move from position 1 to position 2 the triangle was first **rotated** then **translated**. In order to move from position 2 to position 3 the triangle was **reflected**. Here it is necessary to further consider the **2-D transformations** which have taken place.

2-D transformations

There is a range of 2-D transformations which can be applied to shapes, including translation, reflection, rotation and enlargement (see Figure 7.5).

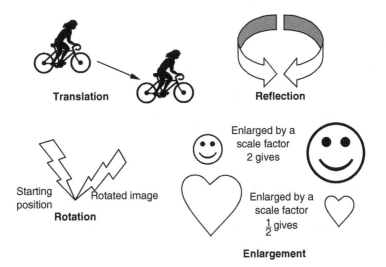

Figure 7.5   2-D transformations

For more information on transformation, see the section on co-ordinates in four quadrants later in this chapter.

- A *translation* takes place when a shape is moved from one place to another just by sliding it (without rotating, reflecting or enlarging). The cyclist (above) has been translated. She has not changed size (enlargement) or orientation (reflection or rotation). She has solely changed position; therefore the two images are congruent.

- When a shape is *reflected* a mirror image is created. The shape and size remain unchanged. Here again the two images are congruent. The position and orientation have changed due to the reflection, but the shape and size remain the same.

- *Rotation* involves a turn around a fixed point. In the above diagram the lightning bolt has been rotated 90° clockwise about the 'point'. Again the two images are congruent. The rotation has caused the orientation to change but not the size or shape.

- In mathematics, *enlargement* can also mean getting smaller! Enlargement is also sometimes called scaling, as in order to change the size it is necessary to decide on a *scale factor* and a centre of enlargement. The scale factor is the number by which you multiply each measurement to achieve the enlargement. If the number is a fraction then the size is reduced. Enlargement is a 2-D transformation which does not result in two congruent images. Often the orientation remains unchanged; however, the size differs.

Similarity

Shapes are said to be similar if all the angles are the same size and the shapes are the same but of a different size, i.e. one is an enlargement of the other.

The two triangles on the opposite page are similar because all their interior angles are the same size. For any triangles, if their interior angles are the same size they must be similar.

Kylie has no understanding of the concept of congruence. In order to develop this concept she will need to study 2-D transformations to establish whether shape, size, position and orientation have been maintained, i.e. to establish whether the resulting shape is congruent or similar.

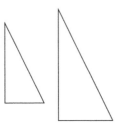

The area of 2-D shapes

REFLECTIVE TASK

Zak is asked to calculate the area of the following shape:

The answer is calculated as 14 cm.

What does this tell you about his understanding of calculating the area of a rectangle?

3cm

4cm

Firstly, it is clear that Zak has recorded the answer as a linear measurement, i.e. in a straight line; hence the answer is expressed in cm. He has not attempted to calculate a 2-D measurement of area. In fact the answer calculated is that of the perimeter (length around the outside) of the shape.

What subject knowledge would you need in order to develop Zak's understanding of the calculation of area?

Rectangles

In order to calculate the area of this rectangle a range of different methods could be used. The simplest would probably be counting squares.

4cm

3cm

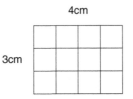

From this it can be seen that the area is 12 cm².

An extension of this method would be to multiply the base by the height. Why does this work?

In the diagram above it can be seen that in order to count squares accurately it is necessary to be systematic. Start in the top left-hand square and count across the top row: 1, 2, 3, 4. Next, move to the second row and repeat: 5, 6, 7, 8. Finally the bottom row: 9, 10, 11, 12. It can be seen from this that the rectangle has an area of three lots of four squares or 3 × 4 cm².

How does this help when calculating the areas of other plane shapes?

Triangles

In a right-angled triangle it is quite straightforward to see that the area must be equal to $\frac{1}{2}$ (base × height).

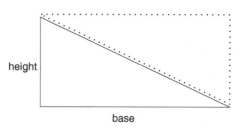

If a second, congruent triangle is positioned next to the right-angled triangle in question, a rectangle is formed. It has already been shown above that the area of a rectangle is equal to base × height; this triangle must therefore have an area equal to one half the area of the rectangle.

Is this true for all triangles?

Let's take an example of a triangle without a right angle.

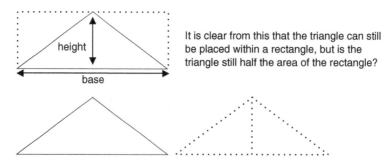

It is clear from this that the triangle can still be placed within a rectangle, but is the triangle still half the area of the rectangle?

By rearranging the triangles above, it can clearly be seen that the two large triangles each have the same area, i.e. half that of the rectangle. This is true for all triangles.

Parallelograms

But what about parallelograms?

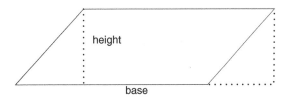

By cutting the parallelogram along the dotted line and repositioning the triangle at the opposite end of the parallelogram, a rectangle is achieved. The height and base measurements of this rectangle are exactly the same as those of the original parallelogram; to calculate the area of a parallelogram is therefore as straightforward as calculating the area of a rectangle, i.e. base × height.

Trapeziums

How does this relate to the trapezium?

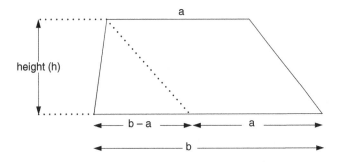

When calculating the area of a trapezium it is necessary to divide it into simpler shapes first. From the diagram above, it can be seen that a trapezium easily divides into a parallelogram and a triangle. Previous sections have already dealt with calculating these areas. The length of the base has been divided into two to enable the calculation to take place.

- The area of the parallelogram is equal to a × h.
- The area of the triangle is equal to $\frac{1}{2}$ (b – a) × h.

- To calculate the area of the trapezium it is necessary to add these two measurements:

$$\text{Area of the trapezium} = ah + \frac{1}{2}(b-a)h$$
$$= ah + \frac{1}{2}bh - \frac{1}{2}ah$$
$$= \frac{1}{2}(a+b)h$$

Circles

A circle is a different kind of plane shape. It is not a polygon, i.e. it does not have straight sides. (Remember 'polygon'? A circle has no knees!)

Calculating areas and circumferences of circles involves the use of the irrational number π (pi). As π is irrational it means the number of decimal places is infinite. The fact that we use an estimation for π in calculations implies that any measure of area or circumference is only an **approximation**.

What is π ?

Pi (π) is found when the circumference of a circle is divided by the diameter:

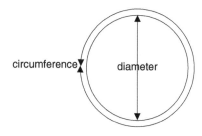

$$\pi = \frac{\text{circumference}}{\text{diameter}}$$

It is approximately equal to 3.141592...

For more information on irrational numbers, see the section on rational and irrational numbers in Chapter 3.

If you use string to measure around a circle and to measure the diameter, and then divide one result by the other, you will obtain an answer as close to 3.14 as the accuracy of the method allows. This will be true for a circle of any size. As the diameter increases, the circumference increases but always maintaining the ratio.

The value of π has been calculated with ever increasing accuracy. The ancient Egyptian 'Rhind Papyrus' has the earliest recording of a value for π of $\frac{258}{81}$ which is about 3.16049. Archimedes (287–212 BCE) calculated π as 3.1419, which is close to today's value. In 1989 the Chudnovsky brothers found π to a billion digits. In 1997 Kanada and Takahashi calculated it to $51\frac{1}{2}$ billion digits.

Yasumasa Kanada continued to pursue pi, and in 2002 he calculated it to 1.2411 trillion places; that's 1,241,100,000,000 places. In 2009, a team led by Daisuke Takahashi calculated pi to double that amount of decimal places.

Using π to calculate the circumference of a circle

Because the value of π is obtained by dividing the circumference (C) by the diameter (d), it can be seen that to find the circumference, π is simply multiplied by the diameter:

$$\text{If } \pi = \frac{C}{d} \text{ then } C = \pi d \text{ or } C = 2\pi r \text{ (where r is equal to the radius).}$$

Using π to calculate the area of a circle

It is possible to show this in a number of ways but the one which probably best models it is shown below. Firstly you have to imagine the circle cut into lots of **sectors**. Next you have to rearrange them as shown. Now imagine the sectors becoming smaller and smaller. As this happens the shape they are forming when rearranged becomes closer and closer to a rectangle, but what are the dimensions of the rectangle? It is quite easy to see that the width of the rectangle is equal to the radius of the circle. The length is also quite straightforward. As half of the sectors are placed facing one direction and the other half are facing the opposite direction, to make the opposite sides of the rectangle, it can be seen that the length is equal to half of the circumference.

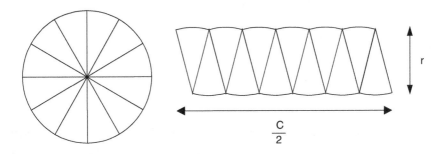

How does this help us calculate the area of the circle?

In order to calculate the area of the circle we simply need to calculate the area of the corresponding rectangle of which we know the dimensions.

$$\text{Area of the rectangle} = \frac{C}{2} \times r$$

We already know that $C = 2\pi r$, so substituting gives:

$$Area = \frac{2\pi r}{2} \times r$$

$$= \pi r \times r$$

$$= \pi r^2$$

Once we can calculate the circumference and area of a circle, sectors and arcs are very straightforward.

Sectors and arcs

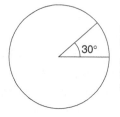

A **sector** is a wedge from the circle (like a slice of pie)

An **arc** is a curved line that forms part of the circumference

To find the arc of this circle we use the fact that we know the angle is 30° and that there are 360° in the full circle. This gives the arc as a fraction of the whole circumference, i.e. $\frac{30}{360}$. If the circumference is multiplied by this fraction the answer is equal to the length of the arc.

$$\text{Length of the arc} = \frac{30}{360} \times 2\pi r$$

$$= \frac{\pi r}{6}$$

The same method is applied to calculating the area of a sector. We know the sector in this case is $\frac{30}{360}$ of the total area of the circle. To find the sector's area the total area is simply multiplied by the fraction that is the sector. In this case:

$$\text{Area of the sector} = \frac{30}{360} \times \pi r^2$$

$$= \frac{\pi r^2}{12}$$

3-D shapes

Beth was asked to identify the number of faces, edges and vertices in the following solids:

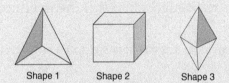

Shape 1   Shape 2   Shape 3

She gave the following answers:

	Faces	Edges	Vertices
Shape 1	4	4	6
Shape 2	6	8	12
Shape 3	8	6	12

What does this tell you about her understanding of defining 3-D shapes?

It is clear that Beth does not fully understand the terms 'face', 'edge' and 'vertex'. What subject knowledge will you need to be able to support her to develop her understanding?

So far, this chapter has focused on 2-D shapes. However, we live in a 3-D world and therefore we need to recognise properties and characteristics of 3-D shapes in order to gain a fuller understanding of spatial concepts.

The shapes shown to Beth are all polyhedra. 'Polyhedron' comes from *poly* meaning 'many' and *hedron* from the Indo-European word meaning 'seat'. Hence, polyhedron means 'many seats'. A polyhedron is a solid formed from flat faces, but what are faces, edges and vertices?

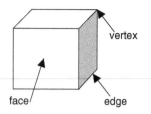

Face – the flat surfaces of solid shapes (i.e. parts of planes).

Edge – the line where two faces join (i.e. the intersection of two plane faces of a solid).

Vertex – the point of face edge intersection of edges.

As with polygons there are some regular polyhedra. Incredibly there are only five regular polyhedra. A polyhedron is defined as regular if all its faces are congruent (regular polygons have the same number of faces meeting at every vertex). This also means that all the angles between the faces (i.e. the dihedral angles) are the same size. This means that the shape will look the same regardless of which face it is 'sitting' on.

The Platonic solids

The five regular polyhedra form a group of solids known as the **Platonic solids**. The five solids are the **regular tetrahedron**, the **cube**, the **regular octahedron**, the **regular dodecahedron** and the **regular icosahedron**. The Platonic solids have been known since the time of the ancient Greeks. They were described by Plato in 350 BCE and hence now bear his name. The fact that there can be only five was proved by Euclid (325–270 BCE).

There is an interesting relationship between the number of faces, edges and vertices of the Platonic solids:

Solid	Faces	Edges	Vertices
Tetrahedron	4	6	4
Cube	6	12	8
Octahedron	8	12	6
Dodecahedron	12	30	20
Icosahedron	20	30	12

From this table the relationship between the number of faces, edges and vertices can be seen:

Faces + Vertices = Edges + 2 or $F + V = E + 2$

This is called **Euler's formula** and applies not only to the Platonic solids (i.e. regular solids) but also to a great many other solids, almost certainly all those that will be encountered within a primary school. Euler's formula is named after Leonhard Euler, who proved this formula in 1735.

Polyhedra are named as consistently as polygons, not only the regular polyhedra but also the irregular ones. In the diagram of **pyramids** below, one of the shapes is a pentahedron (five faces) and the other is a heptahedron (seven faces).

Other polyhedra can be classified together to form particular groups.

Pyramids

Pyramids are solids that have a polygon base and triangular faces. It is easy to decide what to call each pyramid as it takes its name from the shape of its base: for example, a square pyramid or a hexagonal pyramid.

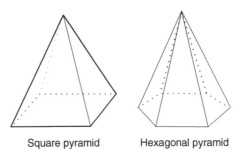

Square pyramid   Hexagonal pyramid

Prisms

Prisms are a different group of solids. They each have a uniform cross-section. This means that if you cut them anywhere along their length, parallel to their base, you will always obtain a shape that is identical to the base shape.

Rectangular prism   Triangular prism

As with pyramids, prisms take their names from the shape of their base, hence the rectangular and triangular prisms above.

Nets

A net is a flat shape that can be folded to form a solid. Any polyhedron has a number of different nets. For example, the cube has 11 possible nets. Three possible cube nets are shown below:

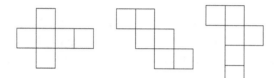

PRACTICAL TASK

Nets for some irregular polyhedra are shown below. For which of the solids are they the nets?

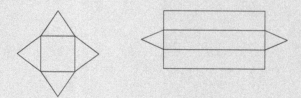

The first is the net of a square pyramid (or pentahedron). The second is the net of a triangular prism (also a pentahedron). Explore the nets of cubes further. Can you find the other eight nets to complete the set of eleven (don't look until you've tried it yourself)? Take care to avoid rotations and reflections. The eight below, together with the three above, form the full set.

Surface area and volume

The surface area of a polyhedron is equal to the sum of the areas of its faces and is measured in square units, e.g. cm². The volume of a solid is the amount of space it takes up. It is measured in cubic units, e.g. cm³.

For more information on how to calculate surface areas of polyhedra, see Chapter 6.

For Beth, developing a greater understanding of the correct mathematical vocabulary of 3-D shapes will ensure accuracy as further spatial concepts are introduced.

Cartesian co-ordinates

This chapter has concentrated on shapes and transformations, but it is also very important to be able to express where in space something is located. This requires a consideration of **Cartesian co-ordinates**.

REFLECTIVE TASK

Sam was asked to plot the following pairs of Cartesian co-ordinates:

(2,1) (2,3) (6,1) (6,3)

He produced the following result:

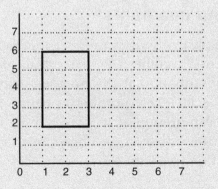

(Continued)

(Continued)

What does this tell you about Sam's understanding of Cartesian co-ordinates in the first quadrant?

Sam does not understand that the first number represents the distance travelled along the x-axis and the second number represents the distance travelled along the y-axis. What subject knowledge do you need to effectively support your development of Sam's understanding?

Cartesian co-ordinates are named after the French philosopher and scientist René Descartes (1596–1650). It is vital that co-ordinates are read correctly, otherwise they are completely inaccurate. The first number (the **abscissa**) always represents the distance along the x-axis (horizontal axis), and the second number (the **ordinate**) the distance travelled along the y-axis (vertical axis). There are many ways of remembering this, e.g. 'bottoms up!', 'along the corridor then up the stairs', OUT – 'Out and UpTo it'.

Sam was working with co-ordinates in the first quadrant only. However, it is important to know that we can work with co-ordinates in four quadrants, and indeed three dimensions. This book will not consider 3-D co-ordinates, but if you are interested there are lots of websites containing a wealth of information.

Co-ordinates in four quadrants

Just as in the first quadrant, the first number represents the distance along the x-axis and the second number the distance along the y-axis. The only difference in four quadrants is that the numbers may be negative. Look at Figure 7.6 and try to decide the co-ordinates before reading on. 2-D transformations can also be represented in this way. It is possible to identify relationships between the sets of co-ordinates of the original shape and its image after transformation (see Figure 7.7).

For Sam, the first thing to learn is the meaning of the co-ordinates in order to support wider study within this area.

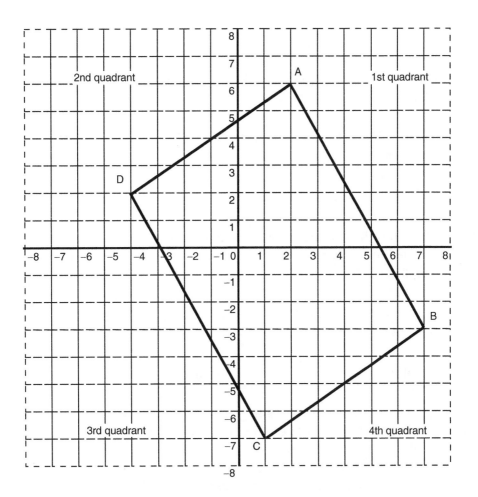

A (2, 6), B (7,–3), C (1,–7), D(–4, 2)

Figure 7.6 Co-ordinates in four quadrants

PRACTICAL TASK (see Figure 7.7, p. 179)

For each of the further images C, D and E, identify the transformation that shape A has undertaken and list the new co-ordinates.

- To create image (C) shape (A) has been enlarged, with the centre of enlargement being (0, 0). The new co-ordinates are:

(0,0) (2,0) (2,2) (4,2) (4,4) (2,4) (2,6) (0,6)

(Continued)

(Continued)

Because shape (A) has been enlarged by a scale factor 2, each co-ordinate has been multiplied by 2.

- To create image (D) shape (A) has been reflected in the x-axis. The new co-ordinates are:

(0,0) (1,0) (1,-1) (2,-1) (2,-2) (1,-2) (1,-3) (0,-3)

The result is that the y value for each of the co-ordinates is now negative, i.e. it has been multiplied by -1. Reflection in the y-axis would result in the x value being multiplied by -1.

- To create image (E) shape (A) has been rotated 180° clockwise (or anticlockwise) about the origin (0,0). The new co-ordinates are:

(0,0) (-1,0) (-1,-1) (-2,-1) (-2,-2) (-1,-2) (-1,-3) (0,-3)

The result here is that both x and y values have been multiplied by -1. This is because the new image is in the 3rd quadrant. If (A) was rotated 90° clockwise about the origin, the x and y values would swap and the new y value would be multiplied by -1. This happens because the orientation changes and the image is in the 4th quadrant. A 270° clockwise rotation about the origin again results in the x and y values swapping, owing to the new orientation, but this time the new x value is multiplied by -1 because the image is in the 2nd quadrant.

Angles

An **angle** is simply a way of describing a measurement of turn. We call its unit of measurement the degree. When two lines meet at a right angle (90°) we call them **perpendicular lines**.

On the other hand, two lines which travel in the same direction but which never meet are called **parallel lines**.

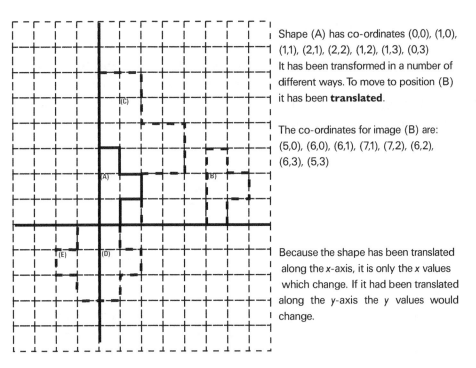

Shape (A) has co-ordinates (0,0), (1,0), (1,1), (2,1), (2,2), (1,2), (1,3), (0,3)

It has been transformed in a number of different ways. To move to position (B) it has been **translated**.

The co-ordinates for image (B) are: (5,0), (6,0), (6,1), (7,1), (7,2), (6,2), (6,3), (5,3)

Because the shape has been translated along the x-axis, it is only the x values which change. If it had been translated along the y-axis the y values would change.

Figure 7.7 2-D transformations represented by co-ordinates in four quadrants

When two straight lines intersect each other, the two angles that lie opposite each other are called **vertically opposite angles**.

Since the lines that are intersecting are straight lines, their angles must add up to 180°. We call the angles that are adjacent to each other on the straight line **supplementary angles**.

Where parallel lines are crossed by a straight line, we not only create vertically opposite angles but also **corresponding angles** which are equal:

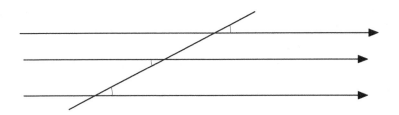

The angles marked in this diagram are alternate angles which are also equal. We can study the concept of angle in two different ways. The first is what we call a 'static' experience. This involves comparing angles with what we know already. For instance, we can look at an angle and decide whether or not it is greater or smaller than a right angle. We can look for the difference in the shape made by two lines or for the difference in direction between the two lines.

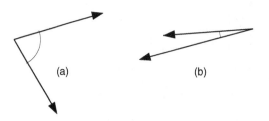

The angle marked in (a) is greater than the angle in (b). The difference in the shape made by the two sets of lines is obvious because of the difference in the direction of the lines.

The second experience we can have when studying the concept of angle is a 'dynamic' experience. This is the preferable option as it lends itself to a more practical approach leading to greater understanding of the concept. For instance, by slowly opening a book we can see the angle between the pages growing as the book opens wider. Similarly if we open and close a door slowly we can see the size of the angle changing.

RESEARCH SUMMARY

Learning about angle in Norway

In Norway, the learning of angle concepts in primary school is carried out as an integrated part of the children's physical activity (Fyhn, 2008). In doing so, the children learn that there are two ways of considering an angle: both as a measurement between two static sides and as the process of change in direction.

Fyhn (2008) used a class climbing trip to research how 12-year-olds develop their understanding of angle. She explains that when climbing your body forms and reforms angles by making different shapes (page 19), taking advantage of the fact that human mathematics is embodied, it is grounded in bodily experience in the world (Lakoff and Nunez, 2000, cited in Fyhn, page 21). She hoped that the children would be able to identify some of these angles (created by the children's joints, the ropes and the climbing wall, floor and roof) and that these in turn could be used as a resource in a later mathematics lesson, because she knew that exploring problems in context supports children to come to grips with formal mathematics (page 20).

The children wrote and drew about their climbing trip and Fyhn analysed their work. In doing so, she identified three levels of understanding: recognition of angles, description of angles and using angles as a contextual tool.

Fyhn saw that within the three levels of recognition, description and contextual tool the children used either narrative or analytical approaches. Her article explains how she intends to develop the children's analytical understanding further next time she teaches angle through climbing.

Two geostrips joined together at one end can create a worthwhile visual and practical experience when we gradually open the strips wider and wider. Playing games which involve turning ourselves in different directions is another example of dynamic geometry. Obviously we must ensure that we understand the link between static and dynamic geometry so that when faced with a 2-D representation we can visualise the rotation involved and understand the measurement of turn.

The instruments we use to measure angles are protractors and angle measurers. The most useful protractor in primary school is the 360° angle measurer, which emphasises the dynamic view of the angle.

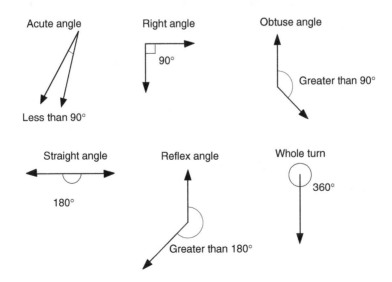

Bearings and compass points

A bearing indicates the direction of one point in relation to another point. It is measured in a clockwise direction from a line which points due north and is always given as a three digit number.

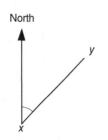

y has a bearing of 045° from *x*.

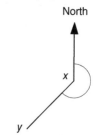

y has a bearing of 240° from *x*.

A SUMMARY OF KEY POINTS

- Polygons are plane shapes with many angles.
- They are named systematically.
- A regular polygon has all sides of equal length and all interior angles of equal size.
- A shape is said to have reflective symmetry if you can fold it so that one half fits exactly on top of the other half.
- A shape is said to have rotational symmetry if it looks the same in different positions when rotated about its centre.
- 2-D transformations include translation, reflection, rotation and enlargement.
- Shapes are congruent if they are the same shape and size, regardless of orientation and position.
- Shapes are similar if all the angles are the same size and the shapes are the same but of a different size, i.e. one is an enlargement of the other.
- Polyhedra are solid shapes with many faces.
- They are named systematically.

- A polyhedron is defined as regular if all its faces are congruent (regular polygons have the same number of faces meeting at every vertex).
- Cartesian co-ordinates can be used to express where something is located in space.
- The dynamic view of angle is fundamental to understanding the concept of angle.

M-LEVEL EXTENSION

Reflect on the arguments concerning the importance of geometry in an increasingly 3-D digital world. What does the need for the development of visual reasoning mean in relation to your planning for 'Shape and space' in the primary school? How can you explain the importance of this aspect to children in terms of real-life applications of geometry?

FURTHER READING

DfE (2011) *Teachers' Standards*. Available at https://www.gov.uk/government/uploads/system/uploads/attachment_data/file/301107/Teachers__Standards.pdf

Hansen, A. (ed.) (2017) *Children's Errors in Mathematics*, 4th edn. London: Sage/Learning Matters. This book tackles mathematical misconceptions in a clear and concise manner. It explains why the misconceptions occur, suggests remediation and supports pre-empting them when planning. There is a very useful chapter on geometry that should support your developing role as a teacher.

Haylock, D. (2014) *Mathematics Explained for Primary Teachers*, 5th edn. London: Sage. As the title suggests, this book explains much of the content of the primary mathematics curriculum. It also addresses key teaching points and gives opportunities to try some self-assessment questions in each area, to further support your subject knowledge development.

Haylock, D. and Cockburn, A. (2017) *Understanding Mathematics for Young Children: A Guide for Teachers of Children 3–7*, 5th edn. London: Sage. This book aims to provide readers with a clearer understanding of the mathematics they will encounter in the classroom. Its focuses include mathematical symbolism and developing appropriate mathematical language.

https://study.sagepub.com/content/subject-knowledge-test-maths

An online self-audit to help identify areas of strength and further targets for development.

http://www.bbc.co.uk/schools/gcsebitesize/maths/

A useful site which, as the name suggests, breaks mathematics into 'bite-sized' pieces.

8

Statistics

Teachers' Standards

A teacher must:

3. Demonstrate good subject and curriculum knowledge

   - have a secure knowledge of the relevant subject(s) and curriculum areas, foster and maintain pupils' interest in the subject, and address misunderstandings
   - demonstrate a critical understanding of developments in the subject and curriculum areas, and promote the value of scholarship

4. Plan and teach well structured lessons

   - impart knowledge and develop understanding through effective use of lesson time
   - promote a love of learning and children's intellectual curiosity
   - contribute to the design and provision of an engaging curriculum within the relevant subject area(s)

8. Fulfil wider professional responsibilities

   - take responsibility for improving teaching through appropriate professional development

Curriculum context

Early Years Foundation Stage

In the Early Years Foundation Stage children count reliably with numbers from 1 to 20, place them in order and say which number is one more or one less than a given number. Using quantities and objects, children add and subtract two single-digit numbers and count on or back to find the answer. They solve problems, including doubling, halving and sharing. Children also use everyday language to compare quantities and objects and to solve problems. This encourages an early introduction to handling data generally as well as leading into the areas of statistics and probability.

National Curriculum programmes of study

During Key Stage 1, children interpret and construct simple pictograms, tally charts, block diagrams and simple tables. They ask and answer simple questions by counting the number of objects in each category and sorting the categories by quantity. Children also ask and answer questions about totalling and comparing categorical data.

In Lower Key Stage 2, children interpret and present discrete and continuous data using appropriate graphical methods, including bar charts and time graphs. They also solve comparison, sum and difference problems using information presented in bar charts, pictograms, tables and other graphs.

In Upper Key Stage 2, children interpret and construct pie charts and line graphs and use these to solve problems. They complete, read and interpret information in tables, including timetables, and calculate and interpret the mean as an average.

Statistics

Introduction

In order to help us make sense of the world around us, we handle the data that surround us and draw information from it. Teachers deal with data often when marking work, target setting, dealing with National Curriculum test results and presenting information for external agencies. This chapter has intentionally used examples that are not specifically related to the data you may come across when teaching. This is because the examples chosen have been designed for you to have a more grounded understanding of the use of statistics in common everyday experiences, just like the data your children will be exploring in mathematics.

Probability came about as we began to make sense of the world around us. We use it to predict the future once we have made some sense of the past. We use probability often in our everyday lives. We forecast the weather according to the probability of rain, and this is based on our knowledge about weather patterns. Many people try to 'beat the odds' when trying to win money in the lottery, football pools and at the races. Although probability is now not formally introduced in the mathematics curriculum until Key Stage 3, it has been left in this chapter for teachers of curricula that still include probability at primary level and for teachers who wish to challenge their own pupils beyond the expectations of Upper Key Stage 2.

This chapter outlines the knowledge and skills that you will need to collect, organise, represent and interpret data, and also addresses issues associated with probability, relating both areas to real-life activities and everyday situations that you will be able to adapt for use in the classroom.

RESEARCH SUMMARY

Price and Raiker (2003) considered teachers' confidence in teaching data handling. They found that teachers' subject knowledge in data handling was a substantial issue and that the teaching of probability was regarded by teachers as particularly difficult. This lack of teacher confidence had a direct impact on pupil confidence and therefore pupil achievement in this area. They also highlighted a possible cause of insufficient and inappropriate in-service training.

Types of data

Discrete and continuous data

We can collect data in two ways: by counting or by measuring. When we can count the data, we call them **discrete data**. That is, there is a discrete category which the item that we have counted can fall into and it is possible to list these. An example of this is favourite pastimes. We can say that 23 people prefer angling and 18 people prefer bungee jumping, but these two pastimes are not connected in any way. In fact it would be very difficult to fish while jumping off a bridge!

Continuous data, however, are measured. These data do not fit into specific discrete categories because the data can be placed anywhere along a line of measurement. It is not possible to list all the outcomes. Imagine, for example, the height of a growing child. At any stage during their life a measurement can be taken. This measurement is an approximation, perhaps to the nearest millimetre. There was a continual growth between the two measurements taken of the child's height at 93 cm and at 106 cm, and an infinite number of heights could have been measured between the time these two heights were recorded.

Another example is a horse steeplechase race. It would be possible to measure the speed at which the horses are travelling at any point during the race. The speed that a horse is travelling around the course and over jumps will change according to whether it is jumping or galloping, the part of the race that is being run or indeed where the horse is placed within the pack.

It is important to understand the difference between discrete and continuous data because the type of data must be known before organising the collection of data. Discrete and continuous data are represented graphically in different ways also. This will be discussed in the next section.

Collecting, recording and representing data

It is possible to collect and record data using a variety of methods. Before deciding on a method of recording data, it is imperative that you know the *type* of data that you are collecting and what you want to find out. Being clear in your mind about what you are collecting and why you are collecting it will mean that you collect only the data you require in a way that is useful for you to record, represent and interpret.

There are two types of data that you may use. You may collect *primary* data in your research. This is collected yourself from the source through a range of techniques. Recording your observations or asking people to complete questionnaires are two such methods. Alternatively you may use *secondary* data in your research. Secondary data have been collected by someone else and can be found in a number of places such as newspapers, books, CD-ROMs, databases on the internet or in historical archives.

This section outlines the various methods of recording data and representing them in tabular and graphical forms.

Tables

Tables are a useful method for both collecting and representing data. Data are easy to compile and read from a table. Let's use the example of favourite pastimes again. Figure 8.1 shows two tables of favourite pastimes. In Table 1, the data were collected using tally marks. Table 2 has the tally marks counted up.

From Table 2, it is easy to read the number of people who state that angling is their favourite pastime. However, Table 1 is, in some ways, easier to gather information from. We can see at a glance which pastime is the most popular because there are more tally marks. It is important to consider the presentation of data in terms of what information needs to be gathered from it.

FAVOURITE PASTIME	NUMBER OF PEOPLE
Angling	ЖЖ ЖЖ ЖЖ ЖЖ |||
Bungee Jumping	ЖЖ ЖЖ ЖЖ |||
Cycling	ЖЖ ЖЖ ЖЖ ЖЖ ЖЖ ||
Fencing	ЖЖ ЖЖ ЖЖ ||
Reading	|||
Rock Climbing	ЖЖ ЖЖ ЖЖ
Playing Cards	
Walking	ЖЖ ЖЖ ||

Table 1

FAVOURITE PASTIME	NUMBER OF PEOPLE
Angling	23
Bungee Jumping	18
Cycling	27
Fencing	17
Reading	3
Rock Climbing	15
Playing Cards	0
Walking	12

Table 2

Figure 8.1 Recording data in tables

Graphs and diagrams

It is often easier to read data from graphs and diagrams rather than from tables when wanting to begin to interpret data and predict from it. The following are the diagrams and graphs that you need to be familiar with. The earlier graphs are not shown here as this book is aimed at your own level of subject knowledge and it is assumed that you are familiar with them. If you are unsure, you can also find them in the companion mathematics book in this series, called *Primary Mathematics: Teaching Theory and Practice* (Learning Matters, 2014).

Block graphs

Block graphs are used to display discrete data. One block can represent one item, or a number of items. It is necessary to have a key to explain how many items each block represents.

Pictograms

Pictograms are used to display discrete data. One picture/symbol can represent one item or a number of items. Again, it is necessary to have a key to explain how many items each symbol represents. It is equally necessary to ensure that each of the pictures/symbols is of a similar size and that if they represent many items then it is clear how many items they represent when they are not whole.

Pictograms are a simple way to record and display a small data set. Pictograms are a great way to introduce children to data representation as they can be entirely

Fruit	Number of children who chose it
Apple	🍎🍎🍎
Pear	🍐🍐🍐🍐
Orange	🍊🍊
Banana	🍌🍌🍌🍌🍌

Example of a simple pictogram

pictoral (so children who have not yet mastered reading can still access learning through pictograms). Children can often interpret pictograms intuitively. For example, if you showed the following to a young child in Reception and asked, 'What fruit did more children like?' they are likely to respond with the correct answer. Higher up the school, pictograms can be a more interesting and impactful way of representing data. More and more, infographics are becoming increasingly used to visually display data and you are likely to have seen many through social media and across the internet.

Bar graphs

Bar graphs are used to display discrete data. The length of each bar represents the number of items (the frequency). Each bar is separate to show that the data are discrete. Bar graphs can be drawn vertically and horizontally.

Bar-line graphs

Bar-line graphs display the same information as bar graphs. Lines are used instead of bars to represent the frequency of the data.

Pie charts

Pie charts are circle graphs cut into sectors. By calculating the fraction of the circle, the percentage of the circle, or the degrees of the circle, it is possible to make each sector. Pie charts are often used to compare proportions.

Line graphs

Line graphs are used to display continuous data. A line graph of the speed of steeplechase horses will rise and fall according to the section of the race they are running. A line graph of a child's height, however, is probably going to increase, as is a graph showing the distance travelled in a car on a journey.

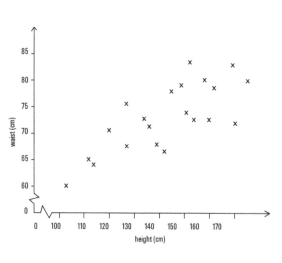

Scattergraph

Scattergraphs

Scattergraphs are used to compare two sets of data. These data can be discrete or continuous.

The example on the right compares the height of Year 5 children with their waist size.

It is possible to make decisions about the correlation between the two sets of data, and lines of best fit. When comparing the data, scattergraphs allow us to draw conclusions about correlations between the two sets of data.

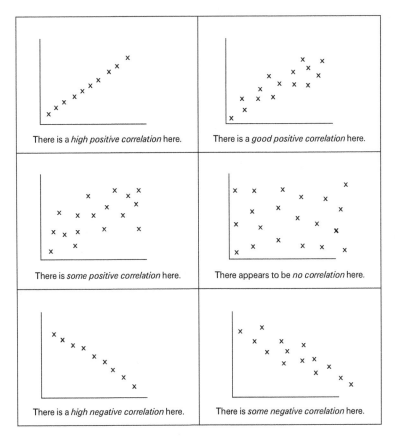

Correlation

Frequency diagrams

Frequency diagrams are used with continuous data. The data are grouped into classes. On the right, there is a frequency diagram of the weight of a class of children in Year 6. In this example there are eight children who weigh less than 50 kg and more than, or equal to, 45 kg.

Weight (kg)	Frequency
30≤W<35	2
35≤W<40	5
40≤W<45	10
45≤W<50	8
50≤W<55	6
55≤W<60	3
60≤W<65	1

Frequency diagram

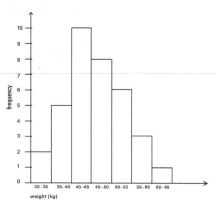

**Histogram showing the weight
of Year 6 pupils**

Upper bound	Cumulative frequency
<35	2
<40	7
<45	17
<50	25
<55	31
<60	34
<65	35

Cumulative frequency diagram

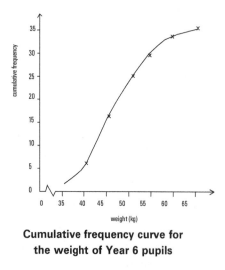

**Cumulative frequency curve for
the weight of Year 6 pupils**

Frequency histogram

Histograms graphically represent continuous data. Unlike a bar graph, the 'bars' of the histogram touch. In each 'bar', the *area* represents the frequency. In this example, the class intervals are the same width, so the heights of the 'bars' are in proportion with their frequencies. Sometimes this is not the case, and you will need to look at the areas of the histogram more carefully.

Cumulative frequency

Sometimes it is necessary to use a **cumulative** frequency. The cumulative frequency diagram here has used the data from above. From this diagram it is easy to read how many pupils weigh less than, say, 55 kg.

It is possible to graph the cumulative frequency data from above in a **curve**. The points of the cumulative data are plotted and then usually joined together with curves (although sometimes line segments are also used).

Interpreting data

Having collected and represented data, it is an equally important skill to be able to interpret the data and predict from it.

If the data were gathered with a specific question in mind, then the main part of the interpretation of the data will be to answer the question originally set. This is certainly a means to an end, where the data collection has been undertaken purely to answer a set question. Often, however, the interpretation of and prediction from data are not that straightforward. We are bombarded with data from many sources every day when watching the television, listening to the news on the radio, or reading newspapers and magazines.

You have probably heard the old adage: 'lies, damned lies and statistics'. Statistics can be used to prove almost anything, if the statistician is clever (or naughty) enough. A graph once 'proved' that babies were indeed brought by storks, because a scatter-graph that had been created showed a high positive correlation between nesting storks and the birthrate in a town suburb! It is therefore necessary, at times, to be sceptical about the data and graphical representations that you are presented with rather than accepting them at face value.

It may be necessary to ask questions about how the data were collected in order to ascertain possible sources of error and the limitations of the data collection. How accurate were the measurements? Were the questions asked openly, or could they have been asked in a misleading way, making the data less accurate? How many people were asked? Did they all respond, or did only the people with the strongest views bother to reply?

Data prediction

Sometimes data can be a powerful resource for predicting likely outcomes based on previous experience. It is possible to identify long-term and short-term features in time-series data. For example, if data were gathered about a steeplechase horse over a number of races, its trainer would be able to begin to build a profile about the horse's strengths and weaknesses. This information could be used to improve the training and the racing of the horse.

It is also possible to make and justify statements about relationships between variables in a sample as the result of a statistical investigation, for example using scattergraphs.

From these populations, it is possible to make statistically based inferences about whole populations, and even confidently express reasoned opinions from the media.

Finding and using the mean and other central measures

PRACTICAL TASK

Visit the BBC Weather website at http://www.bbc.co.uk/weather/. Select a city of your choice and look under the 'more' tab at 'Average Conditions'. What do you notice about the data that the BBC gives you? Think about how the data might be useful to you and to others. How easy is it to make sense of the data when it is presented in this way?

The mean

The **mean**, or **arithmetic mean** (which is its correct name), is the most common type of **average** that is used. It is used in many everyday situations, such as monthly temperature, runs per over in cricket and student marks. It is found by adding up all the components in a set of data and dividing the sum by the number of components in the set.

For example, the mean temperature in a country in the southern hemisphere in February is 19°C. The days within February vary quite a lot. Look at this list of temperatures:

20, 21, 19, 17, 16, 18, 17, 20, 19, 18, 21, 21, 18, 19, 18, 20, 21, 22, 20, 19, 19, 15, 16, 18, 20, 22, 21, 20

To find the mean temperature, the temperatures are added together, and then divided by the number of days in the month. The sum of the temperatures is 535. When divided by the number of days in the month (28), the mean temperature is 19.1°C.

It is also possible to calculate the mean from a frequency distribution (see below). This is an easier method of finding the mean if there is a large amount of data.

Temperature (°C)	Frequency	Temp. × Frequency
x	f	fx
15	1	15
16	2	32
17	2	34
18	5	90
19	5	95
20	6	120
21	5	105
22	2	44
	28	535

$$\text{Mean temperature} = \frac{\Sigma fx}{\Sigma f}$$
$$= \frac{\text{total of (temperature×frequency)}}{\text{total number of days in the month}}$$

Σ is **sigma**. It means 'the sum of'.

The median

The **median** is the middle value in a set of data. In order to find the median, the data must first be put in order:

15, 16, 16, 17, 17, 18, 18, 18, 18, 18, 19, 19, 19, 19, 19, 20, 20, 20, 20, 20, 20, 21, 21, 21, 21, 21, 22, 22

Then it is necessary to find the middle value. You can do this by dividing the number of components in the set by two, or by counting in from the end values until you meet in the middle. In this example, there are 28 values. Because 28 is an even number, it is possible to divide the set of data into two evenly. Therefore the middle is between two values. It happens that both of the values it lies between are 19, so the median is 19. Had it fallen between two values that were not the same, then the mean of those two numbers would be taken as the median. Had the set comprised the number of days in February in a leap year, the number of values present would have been 29. The median would have been the 15th value.

$$\text{The position of the median} = \frac{(n+1)}{2}$$
$$= \frac{28+1}{2}$$
$$= 14.5$$

The mode

The **mode** is the value that occurs most commonly in any set of data. In the temperature example, the temperature that occurs most commonly is 20°C. There were six days that reached 20 degrees, so the mode for this set of data is 20. Other frequent temperatures are 18, 19 and 21. Each of these occurred five times. Had 20°C also occurred five times in February (instead of six), then there would have been four modes for this set of data.

Why are the mean, median and mode sometimes different from each other? In our example, the mean and median of the February temperatures are 19°C. The mode, however, is 20°C. If you look at the data carefully, you will note that there was one cooler day where the temperature was recorded at only 15°C. This unusually cool temperature for the month has meant that the extreme value has had an impact on calculating the mean.

The range

The **range** gives a measure of the spread of a set of data. In this case the temperatures range from 15°C to 22°C and so the range is calculated by finding the difference (22–15) which is 7°C. You can find out more about the range and measures of spread in the next section.

When are the mean, median and mode best used?

The mean is the most common measure of average. It is used to compare different sets of data. For example, now that we have the mean temperature of February in one country, we could compare it with other countries' mean temperatures or even other months of the same country to look at the climate, perhaps with a view to going on holiday.

It is useful to look at the median when working with small sets of data. The median is not affected by extreme values within the data, such as the 15°C in the temperature example.

Sometimes, it is not appropriate to calculate the mean or the median. For example, if a group of people were planning a trip to the country discussed above, then it would be sensible to look at the most common temperatures, or the modal temperatures. The mode of the temperatures above is 20°C. So, it would make sense to pack mostly clothes that could be worn at 20°C, with fewer for 15°C.

Finding and using measures of spread to compare distributions

If we were planning a trip to the country where these temperatures were taken, we would want to look at the **range** of temperatures to ensure that we packed appropriate clothing for the holiday outlined above. It would also be possible to compare the range of these temperatures with the range of temperatures from another country to look at the spread over the month of February. If we were looking for somewhere to take a light bag, we might want to select a country that has a narrow spread of high temperatures. The use of the range is the simplest method of finding and using a measure of spread to compare distributions.

Box and whisker diagrams

It is possible to use a **box and whisker diagram** to compare distributions graphically. This involves calculating the median as well as two other measures, called **quartiles**.

15, 16, 16, 17, 17, 18, 18, 18, 18, 18, 19, 19, 19, 19, 19, 20, 20, 20, 20, 20, 20, 21, 21, 21, 21, 21, 22, 22

Above are the temperatures of a country in the southern hemisphere in February. In the previous section we calculated the median by finding the middle temperature. We will use the same technique to find the quartiles. To find the **lower quartile**, it is necessary to ascertain one quarter of the data. To find the **upper quartile**, it is necessary to ascertain three quarters of the data.

There are 28 values in this example. Because 28 is a multiple of 4, it is possible to divide the set of data into four evenly. Therefore each of the quartiles lies between two values:

15, 16, 16, 17, 17, 18, 18 | 18, 18, 18, 19, 19, 19, 19 | 19, 20, 20, 20, 20, 20, 20 | 21, 21, 21, 21, 21, 22, 22

If we look at the lower quartile, it happens that both values it lies between are 18, so the lower quartile is 18. The upper quartile, however, has fallen between two values that were not the same: 20 and 21. The mean of those two numbers is taken as the upper quartile, so the upper quartile is 20.5.

$$\text{The position of the lower quartile} = \frac{(n+1)}{4} = \frac{28+1}{4} = 7.25$$

$$\text{The position of the upper quartile} = \frac{3(n+1)}{4} = \frac{3(28+1)}{4} = \frac{87}{4} = 21.75$$

It is also possible to calculate the **interquartile range**. The range can be affected by extreme values, so using the interquartile range to compare sets of data removes the extreme values. The interquartile range is the range between the upper and lower quartiles.

Interquartile range = upper quartile – lower quartile

$$= 20.5 - 18$$

$$= 2.5$$

Having found the quartiles and the median, it is possible to graphically represent these data in a box and whisker diagram:

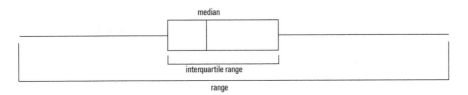

Figure 8.2 Box and whisker diagram

The interquartile range covers 50% of the data and each 'whisker' represents 25% of the data. When two or more box and whisker diagrams are placed together, it is possible to make comparisons between them more easily than when looking at the raw data.

The probability scale

We use probability to predict the likelihood of a future event happening. In everyday discussion we use words such as 'certain' and 'unlikely' when we are talking about upcoming events. We can place these words on a **probability scale** like this:

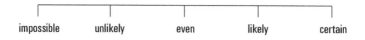

| impossible | unlikely | even | likely | certain |

In mathematics this probability scale becomes more formalised as fractions, percentages or decimals replace these words. For example, an event that is certain to happen has a probability of 1, or 100%, whereas an event that has an even chance of happening (such as tossing a coin to get a head) has a probability of $\frac{1}{2}$, 50% or 0.5:

0	$\frac{1}{4}$	$\frac{1}{2}$	$\frac{3}{4}$	1
0%	25%	50%	75%	100%
0.0	0.25	0.5	0.75	1.0

How can we identify the probability of an event?

It is only possible to make an objective statement about the probability of an event if you have some prior knowledge about the event. For example, it would not be possible to make a statement about the probability of iguanas in South America mating this month unless you know about iguanas in South America, or you know something about the mating season of iguanas and you know about the weather in South America.

There are three ways that you can have some knowledge about an event:

- The first is based on *prior knowledge*: it may be possible to ascertain previous statistical data and work from this. This is used most often in the everyday world. This type of probability is used in calculating insurance premiums, choosing investments and forecasting the weather.

- The second is to undertake an experiment to re-enact an event. This often occurs in the fields of science and mathematics where many experiments take place to ensure the safety of a chemical, introduced species, or vehicle air bags, etc. The more the experiment is undertaken, the closer to the expected outcome we should be. The *experimental probability* (also known as relative frequency) can be calculated by dividing the number of outcomes by the total number of trials.

$$\textbf{experimental probability} = \frac{\textbf{number of successful outcomes}}{\textbf{total number of trials}}$$

- The third is to use the theoretical knowledge about the event to predict an outcome. We know that there is an even chance of getting a 'tail' when we toss a coin, because there are two possible, even outcomes before tossing the coin: a head and a tail. The *theoretical probability* can be calculated by dividing the number of actual outcomes by the total number of possible outcomes.

$$\textbf{theoretical probability} = \frac{\textbf{number of successful outcomes}}{\textbf{total number of possible outcomes}}$$

If we toss one coin, we can get a head or a tail. The probability of getting a head is $\frac{1}{2}$.

The probability of getting a tail is $\frac{1}{2}$ also.

$$\frac{1}{2} + \frac{1}{2} = 1$$

REFLECTIVE TASK

If we toss the coin once and get a head, what is the probability of throwing a head the next time?

The probability of throwing a head again is $\frac{1}{2}$. The probability does not change depending on what has gone before. Every time we toss the coin, there is still an even chance of tossing a head or a tail. The events are **mutually exclusive**.

If we throw a die, the possible outcomes are 1, 2, 3, 4, 5 or 6. The probability of throwing any one of these numbers is $\frac{1}{6}$.

$$\frac{1}{6} + \frac{1}{6} + \frac{1}{6} + \frac{1}{6} + \frac{1}{6} + \frac{1}{6} = 1$$

Just as with the coin tossing, any prior throws of the die do not have an impact on the probability of throwing a 1, 2, 3, 4, 5 or 6 in the next throw. Again, the events are mutually exclusive.

The probabilities of all the possible mutually exclusive events always add up to 1.

What is the difference between theoretical and experimental probability?

In the previous section we talked about three ways of making an informed judgement about the probability of an event happening. Two of these were theoretical and experimental probability.

PRACTICAL TASK

Toss a coin. Record in an efficient way whether you get a head or a tail. Keep doing this for about a minute. If a number of you are working together, use your own coins and add the number of times you each tossed a head and a tail at the end to carry out a larger experiment.

Prior to starting, what did you expect your outcome to be? If you thought that the number of times you tossed a head would be the same as the number of times you tossed a tail, you were using theoretical probability that tells you the probability of throwing a tail or a head is even. You have now found that the experimental probability is not as accurate as you may originally have thought! You may toss three or four heads in a row, or even more, but every time you toss the coin, the probability of getting a head is still $\frac{1}{2}$. The more times you toss the coin (in other words, undertake the experiment), the closer you will get to the expected outcome.

REFLECTIVE TASK

Tamine in your class complains that she does not like a maths game you have set them to play. To start, she needs to throw a six and she complains that throwing a six is harder than any other number.

What knowledge do you need to have in order to help Tamine to understand about the probability of throwing a six?

You will need to know that there are six possible outcomes when throwing a die. These outcomes are 1, 2, 3, 4, 5 or 6. You will also need to know that there is only one successful outcome when throwing a six, because the die has only one six on it. So, the theoretical probability of throwing a six, written as $P(6)$, is $\frac{1}{6}$. This also means, therefore, that Tamine has a probability of $\frac{5}{6}$ of *not* throwing a six. (This can be calculated by $1 - P(6)$, which is $1 - \frac{5}{6} = \frac{1}{6}$. It is also important that you understand the difference between theoretical and experimental probability, because every time the die is thrown it is mutually exclusive of any other throw, meaning that at every single throw Tamine still has a probability of $\frac{1}{6}$ of getting a six.

When do I add two probabilities?

Let's keep working with a die. Imagine that you change the rules for Tamine in the above example. The rule is now that the child has to throw a 2 *or* a 6 to start. Does this make the game easier or harder to begin? Why?

Yes, it makes the game easier to begin because you can see that throwing a 2 or a 6 is more likely than throwing just a 6. Looking at this mathematically, in terms of probability, the probability of throwing a 6 is $\frac{1}{6}$. The probability of throwing a 2 is also $\frac{1}{6}$.

The probability of throwing a 2 or 6 on a die is:

$$P(2\,or\,6) = P(2) + P(6) = \frac{1}{6} + \frac{1}{6} = \frac{2}{6} = \frac{1}{3}$$

When two mutually exclusive events (A and B) take place, the probability that either happens is:

$$P(A \text{ or } B) = P(A) + P(B)$$

What about throwing two coins?

REFLECTIVE TASK

You are undertaking a probability experiment in class with a group of Year 5 and 6 children where they are tossing two coins and looking at the outcomes. They have decided that there are three possible outcomes: they could toss two heads, a head and a tail, or two tails. They have decided that because there are three possible outcomes, the probability of tossing any of these combinations is $\frac{1}{3}$.

What knowledge will you need in order to help the children in their mathematical understanding?

In the examples above we have worked with mutually exclusive events. We will now explore what happens when we work with **two independent events**. It is often useful to use a systematic way to record the possible outcomes of two independent events. We will use coins again in this example, but we will be tossing two coins at a time.

When we toss two coins there are indeed three possible outcomes: two heads, a head and a tail, or two tails. The pupils' logic falls down only when they assume that each of these possible outcomes has **the same chance** of being thrown.

We can use a number of systematic methods to record what happens when two coins are tossed. We can list the outcomes, make a two-way table, or a tree diagram.

Simply listing the outcomes for this example is straightforward because there are only two outcomes for *each* of the coins. Coin 1 can give a head or a tail, and Coin 2 can give a head or a tail. This listing shows the possible outcomes:

Coin 1	Coin 2
H	H
H	T
T	H
T	T

We could also use a two-way table to list the possible outcomes:

		Coin 2	
		Head (H)	Tail (T)
Coin 1	Head (H)	HH	HT
	Tail (T)	TH	TT

Finally, we could use a tree diagram to list the possible outcomes:

If we follow through each of the branches on the tree diagram, we see the possible outcomes are:

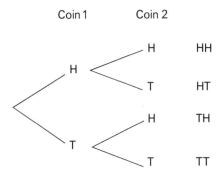

Using any of these methods of recording the possible outcomes, we can see that there are *four* possible outcomes: HH, HT, TH and TT. Of course, when we are tossing the two coins at the same time, we cannot tell the difference between an HT and a TH. From these diagrams it is possible to deduce that the probability of tossing two heads is $\frac{1}{4}$, the probability of tossing two tails is $\frac{1}{4}$ and the probability of tossing a head and a tail (or a tail and a head) is $\frac{2}{4}$ or $\frac{1}{2}$. All these probabilities add up to 1.

We can explain these probabilities in another way. We already know that the probability of tossing a head or a tail on *one* coin is $\frac{1}{2}$. We use this information in order to work out the probability of the possible outcomes of tossing two coins:

The probability of tossing two heads (a head and a head) =

$$P(H) \times P(H) = \frac{1}{2} \times \frac{1}{2} = \frac{1}{4}$$

The probability of tossing two tails (a tail and a tail) =

$$P(T) \times P(T) = \frac{1}{2} \times \frac{1}{2} = \frac{1}{4}$$

When two *independent* events (A and B) occur, then the probability that A and B will *both* happen is:

$$P(A \text{ and } B) = P(A) \times P(B)$$

Now the same rule follows for tossing a head and a tail (or a tail and a head):

The probability of tossing a head and a tail =

$$P(H) \times P(T) = \frac{1}{2} \times \frac{1}{2} = \frac{1}{4}$$

or

The probability of tossing a tail and a head =

$$P(T) \times P(H) = \frac{1}{2} \times \frac{1}{2} = \frac{1}{4}$$

But, because these two possible outcomes look the same when the coins are tossed, we can add the probabilities together:

$$P(H \text{ and } T) \text{ or } P(T \text{ and } H) = \frac{1}{4} + \frac{1}{4} = \frac{2}{4} = \frac{1}{2}.$$

REFLECTIVE TASK

A game for children requires them to place ten counters anywhere they choose along a number track from 2 to 12:

2	3	4	5	6	7	8	9	10	11	12

The children then take turns to roll two dice, adding the totals on the dice. If the square with the sum on it has a counter, the child can remove it. The winner is the child who is first to remove all their counters.

The children place their counters on their favourite numbers, and get frustrated when they cannot throw some of the numbers at the extremes of the number track very often.

What knowledge do you need in order to explain this to the children?

Using a systematic method of recording, we can look at all the ways it is possible to throw each of the sums:

Sum	Possible throws (dice 1+dice 2)	No. of possible ways to make the sum	Probablity of throwing the sum
2	1+1	1	$\frac{1}{36}$
3	1+2,2+1	2	$\frac{2}{36}=\frac{1}{18}$
4	1+3,2+2,3+1	3	$\frac{3}{36}=\frac{1}{12}$
5	1+4,2+3,3+2,4+1	4	$\frac{4}{36}=\frac{1}{9}$
6	5+1,4+2,3+3,2+4,5+1	5	$\frac{5}{36}$
7	1+6,2+5,3+4,4+3,5+2,6+1	6	$\frac{6}{36}=\frac{1}{6}$
8	2+6,3+5,4+4,5+3,6+4	5	$\frac{5}{36}$
9	3+6,4+5,5+4,6+3	4	$\frac{4}{36}=\frac{1}{9}$
10	4+6,5+5,6+4	3	$\frac{3}{36}=\frac{1}{12}$
11	5+6,6+5	2	$\frac{2}{36}=\frac{1}{18}$
12	6+6	1	$\frac{1}{36}$
		36	1

We can see from this chart that the number that is most likely to be thrown is 7 and the numbers that are least likely to be thrown are 2 and 12.

It is possible to use a two-way table to demonstrate this as well:

Die 2

+	1	2	3	4	5	6
1	2	3	4	5	6	7
2	3	4	5	6	7	8
3	4	5	6	7	8	9
4	5	6	7	8	9	10
5	6	7	8	9	10	11
6	7	8	9	10	11	12

Die 1

REFELECTIVE TASK

You have explained to the children all the ways it is possible to throw each of the sums and you think they understand the probability of throwing the different totals.

The next time they play, some of the children put *all ten* of their counters on the number seven and then get despondent when they do not win.

What knowledge do you need in order to explain to them why they were not likely to win?

Although 7 is the most likely number to be thrown $\left(P(7)=\frac{1}{6}\right)$, the probability of throwing a number that was not 7 was much higher $\left(P(not\,7)=\frac{5}{6}\right)$. So those children who put all their counters on 7 were throwing their dice against the odds. These are the same odds as when Tamine tried to throw a 6 in the task earlier in this chapter.

PRACTICAL TASK

Play this game with your friends. Before you begin, how would you arrange your ten counters on the number track? Who won? Why? Have another go. Why is it different this time? Can you explain this in terms of theoretical probability and experimental probability?

A SUMMARY OF KEY POINTS

- Data can be grouped into two categories: *discrete data* (that is counted) and *continuous data* (that is measured).

- There are different methods used to record and represent discrete and continuous data.

- The *arithmetic mean* is the most common type of average that is used. It is usually referred to simply as the *mean*. The *median* is the middle value in a set of data when it is in order. The *mode* is the value that occurs most commonly in a set of data.

- The *range* can be used to find the measure of spread to compare distributions. The *quartiles* are also useful in this comparison.

- There are three ways to begin to consider the probability of an event occurring: the first is based on *prior knowledge*, the second is undertaking an *experiment* and the third is to use *theoretical knowledge* about the event.

- The probabilities of all the possible mutually exclusive events always add up to 1.

- When two *mutually exclusive events* (A and B) take place, the probability that either happens is: P(A or B) = P(A) + P(B).

- When two *independent events* (A and B) occur, the probability that A and B will both happen is: P(A and B) = P(A) × P(B).

M-LEVEL EXTENSION

You may wish to challenge yourself to undertake extended study in the area of data-handling and probability, or to explore the teaching of this aspect further. If you know that data is an area for development in your own mathematical subject knowledge, you may wish to consider undertaking the following suggestions.

Firstly, think about whether your primary concern is with your own knowledge and understanding of handling data and probability. If it is, then this will have an impact on the confidence and speed with which you can teach handling data

(Continued)

(Continued)

and other curriculum topics that require you to manipulate data. It will also impact on the way that you can interpret the data you are presented with as a teacher in the media and in policy documents and discussion papers. In order to help you develop this area of mathematics, you may need to think about what data you use in your everyday life. To begin, look at where graphs are used. Have a look in politically motivated magazines, the newspaper, and the news. Begin to think about those graphs presented to you in a more analytical way, according to the following questions:

- What information is this graph showing me?
- Is it the information I want it to show me?
- Have the data been collected in a valid, reliable way?
- Is the graph misleading in any way?
- Is this the best way to present this type of data to me?
- Is there anything missing that I would have liked to know?

There will also be opportunity in your role as a teacher for you to present data to colleagues and parents. Think about the best way to present this data. Should it be presented in tabular or graphical form? If you decide to use a graph, which best represents your work?

Finally, try to familiarise yourself with many different sources of data, both primary and secondary. Knowing where to look to support your own research for teaching or for the children's work will strengthen your subject knowledge and in turn the confidence with which you teach.

If you are confident in your own knowledge and understanding of handling data but it is the pedagogical knowledge you are less confident with, refer to the companion book in this series entitled *Primary Mathematics: Teaching, Theory and Practice* (Learning Matters, 2014) and to the suggested Further Reading below.

FURTHER READING

Cook, H. (2007) *Mathematics for Primary and Early Years: Developing Subject Knowledge,* 2nd edn. London: SAGE. This book gives even coverage to the National Curriculum subjects. It has a useful introduction that considers why people may have concerns about learning mathematics and how you may overcome these through thinking about what kind of learner you are.

DfE (2011) *Teachers' Standards*. Available at https://www.gov.uk/government/uploads/system/uploads/attachment_data/file/301107/Teachers__Standards.pdf

Hansen, A. (2008) *Primary Mathematics: Extending Knowledge in Practice*. Exeter: Learning Matters. This book offers classroom-based case studies that consider some of the most difficult areas of the primary mathematics curriculum to teach. As well as considering pedagogical issues, it also discusses the subject knowledge required by the teacher to teach the curriculum effectively.

Haylock, D. (2014) *Mathematics Explained for Primary Teachers*, 5th edn. London: Sage. As the title suggests, this book explains much of the content of the primary mathematics curriculum. It also addresses key teaching points and gives opportunities to try some self-assessment questions in each area, to further support your subject knowledge development.

Price, R. and Raiker, A. (2003) Is Teacher Confidence a Factor in the Effective Teaching of Data Handling? *Topic*, 29: 7–11.

Self-assessment questions

Chapter 2 – Number: place value, addition, subtraction, multiplication and division

1. Use the order of precedence of the operations (BODMAS) to calculate the following:

$$30 \div 6 + 4 \times 7 - \frac{1}{4} \text{of} 16 + (12 - 8)$$

2. In which situations can Gelosia multiplication be used?

3. What are the three laws of arithmetic?

4. What makes up the real number system?

Chapter 3 – Number: fractions, decimals and percentages

1. Reduce these fractions to their simplest forms:

   (a) $\frac{9}{18}$ (b) $\frac{14}{62}$ (c) $\frac{78}{126}$ (d) $\frac{25}{5}$

2. What are the answers to:

   (a) $\frac{1}{2} + \frac{5}{7}$ (b) $\frac{3}{5} + \frac{2}{6}$

   (c) $\frac{9}{11} - \frac{1}{3}$ (d) $\frac{3}{4} - \frac{1}{12}$

   (e) $\frac{1}{5} \times \frac{3}{4}$ (f) $\frac{3}{10} \times \frac{1}{9}$

   (g) $\frac{1}{9} \div \frac{2}{3}$ (h) $\frac{4}{7} \div \frac{21}{24}$

3. Convert the following to percentages:

  (a) $\dfrac{2}{5}$ (b) $\dfrac{6}{10}$ (c) $\dfrac{1}{8}$

4. Calculate the following:

  (a) The VAT (at 20%) on £68 (b) 75% of 24 (c) 60% of 80

5. Solve the following inequalities:

  (a) $3x \geq 15$ (b) $-3x \geq 9$ (c) $4x + 3 < 18$

6. Write down the following in standard form:

  (a) 300 (b) 328 000 (c) 7942.8 (d) 0.259

Chapter 4 – Mathematical language, reasoning and proof

1. (a) Prove that the sum of the interior angles of a quadrilateral is always equal to 360°. (You may assume the sum of the angles of a triangle.)

  (b) Suggest an approach to this in which children use inductive thinking.

2. Prove that (a) the product of two even numbers is even, and (b) the product of two odd numbers is odd.

3. Prove that the product of three consecutive numbers is even.

4. Prove by exhaustion that there are only six ways of listing the letters a, b and c.

5. Find counter-examples to refute these assertions:

  (a) Multiplying makes a number larger.

  (b) If a shape has rotational symmetry, it also has reflective symmetry.

  (c) If a and b are both factors of x, then either a is a factor of b, or b is a factor of a.

6. Prove that for any chord, AB, angles â and b̂ are equal. List any assumptions you make.

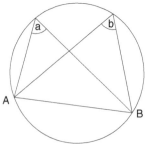

7. List three standard methods of proof that could be used in primary schools.

8. What are the three ways in which we can represent mathematical ideas?

9. What do the following abbreviations mean?

   (a) OE

   (b) ME

10. Give three examples of each of the following:

    (a) Words that have the same meaning in ME and OE.

    (b) Words that have a different meaning in ME from OE.

    (c) Words that have an ME meaning only.

Chapter 5 – Algebra, equations, functions and graphs

1. Simplify the following expressions:

   (a) $5n^2 + 6n - n^2 + 4 - 2n + 1$ (b) $(pq)^2 + p^2q + 4p^2q^2 - 3p(qp) + pq^2$

2. Find the general term for each of these sequences:

(a) Position	1	2	3	4	5
Term	2	5	8	11	14
(b) Position	1	2	3	4	5
Term	4	8	12	16	20

3. Solve the following pairs of simultaneous equations:

   (a) $a - 3b = 1$ (b) $2a - 3b = 4$

   $a + 2b = 11$ $a + 2b = 9$

4. Find the gradients and the y-intercepts of the graphs of the following equations:

   (a) $2y = 6x + 4$ (b) $x + 2y = 4$

5. Extension question.

   Find the general term for the following sequence:

position (n)	1	2	3	4	5
term	−1	4	11	20	31

6. What is a conjecture?

7. What different methods can be used to solve simultaneous linear equations?

8. What is a function?

Chapter 6 – Measures

1. The weight of an average man is 72 kg. What will it be on the moon?

2. The volume of a box is 400 cubic centimetres. What is its capacity?

3. What are the three important stages of development in children's under-standing of measurement identified by the National Curriculum?

4. Name the two different systems of units of measurement used in the UK.

5. The SI determines the units of measurement in the metric system. What does SI stand for?

6. Which aspect of measurement uses the same units in both systems?

7. Complete the following table to show the units of measurement:

	Metric	Imperial
Weight (mass)		
Volume		
Capacity		
Length		
Area		

8. Complete the following approximate equivalences:

Metric	Imperial
28 g	2.2 1b
16 cm³	35 cubic feet
570 ml	
1 L	
	1 inch
	1 foot
6.5 cm²	
	11 square feet

9. The following formulae give the volumes of which regular 3-D shapes?

   (a) $\frac{1}{3}\pi r^2 h$

   (b) $\frac{1}{2}(l \times b \times h)$

   (c) $l \times b \times h$

   (d) $\pi r^2 h$

10. Which formulae would you use to calculate the surface area of the following?

   (a) A cube

   (b) A circle

Chapter 7 – Geometry

1. How many different quadrilaterals can you name which have at least the following characteristics?

   - Opposite sides equal in length and parallel
   - Opposite angles equal
   - Diagonals bisect each other

2. Find the area of the following triangle:

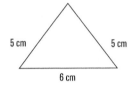

3. Put these angles in order, draw them and classify them as acute, obtuse, or reflex: 212°, 62°, 87°, 134°, $\frac{1}{4}$ turn, $\frac{7}{8}$ of a turn, 23°.

4. A new hopscotch game is to be painted on a playground. On the plan the game is 2 cm wide and 7 cm long. The game on the playground will be similar to the one on the plan. If the playground game is to be 60 cm wide, how long will it be?

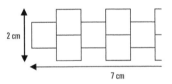

5. Add two squares to each of these shapes to make them have exactly two lines of symmetry.

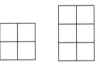

6. Add two squares to each of the following shapes to make them have rotational symmetry of order 4.

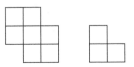

7. (a) Hexominoes are formed when six identical squares are joined contiguously, i.e. they are touching along at least one side, not just corner to corner. How many different, i.e not congruent, hexominoes are there? (Clue: there are more than 11 as we already know that 11 of them form nets for the cube.)

   (b) Applying consistent naming for polyhedra, what would be an alternative name for the cube?

8. Thinking about 2-D shapes:

   (a) Name four different types of triangle.

   (b) Name four different types of quadrilateral.

   (c) Name four transformations that can be applied to 2-D shapes.

9. In describing 3-D shapes, define the following terms:

   (a) Face

   (b) Edge

   (c) Vertex

10. In which quadrants would the following Cartesian co-ordinates be?

   (a) (2, −6)

   (b) (−4, 7)

   (c) (2, 4)

   (d) (−3, −4)

Chapter 8 – Statistics

1. Decide whether these groups of data are discrete or continuous:

   (a) The population of a city.

   (b) A child's height.

   (c) The speed of a car travelling along the motorway.

   (d) The frequency of the word 'broomstick' in a Harry Potter book.

2. A scattergraph showed a good positive correlation between the number of storks seen nesting in a town and the number of babies born. What does this tell you about the possibility of 'storks delivering babies'?

3. The following are two sets of marks from the same group of children. The first set is from a mathematics test and the second from an English test. Both tests were marked out of 20. The marks have been put in order for you.

Maths: 5, 7, 8, 8, 9,10, 10, 11, 12, 12, 12, 12, 13, 13, 14, 15, 15, 15, 16, 16, 17, 17, 17, 18, 18, 18, 18, 19, 19, 20

English: 3, 5, 5, 7, 8, 8, 9, 9, 10, 10, 10, 10, 11, 12, 12, 13, 13, 14, 14, 14, 14, 14, 15, 15, 16, 17, 17, 17, 18, 19

(a) Which test did the children tend to score better in? How do you know?

(b) Calculate the mean, median and mode for each set of data if you have not already done so.

(c) Work out the range and interquartile range for both sets of data.

(d) What reasons might you think of to explain the difference in test scores?

4. Consider the throwing of a regular six-sided die and the tossing of a coin. What is the probability that:

(a) an even number and a head are shown?

(b) a multiple of 3 and a tail are shown?

(c) a 1 and a head are shown?

(d) a multiple of 7 and a head are shown?

5. List four ways of displaying discrete data.

6. List four ways of displaying continuous data.

7. Define the following terms:

(a) Mean

(b) Median

(c) Mode

(d) Range

(e) Quartiles

8. What are the three possible ways of identifying the probability of an event?

Answers to self-assessment questions

Chapter 2 – Number: place value, addition, subtraction, multiplication and division

1. $30 \div 6 + 4 \times 7 - \dfrac{1}{4} \text{of} 16 + (12 - 8)$ Brackets

    $30 \div 6 + 4 \times 7 - \dfrac{1}{4} \text{of} 16 + 4$ of

    $30 \div 6 + 4 \times 7 - 4 + 4$ Division

                                  Multiplication

    $5 + 28 - 4 + 4$ Addition

    33 Subtraction

2. Gelosia multiplication can be used to multiply whole numbers and decimals.

3. The three laws of arithmetic are the commutative, the associative and the distributive. Addition and multiplication are both commutative and associative. Multiplication is distributive over addition and subtraction. Division is right distributive over addition and subtraction.

4. The set of rational numbers (all that can be written as fractions) and the set of irrational numbers (those that cannot be expressed in fractional form) make up the real number system.

Chapter 3 – Number: fractions, decimals and percentages

1. (a) $\frac{1}{2}$ (b) $\frac{7}{31}$

   (c) $\frac{13}{21}$ (d) 5

Answers to self-assessment questions

2. (a) $\dfrac{1}{2}+\dfrac{5}{7}=\dfrac{7}{14}+\dfrac{10}{14}=\dfrac{17}{14}=1\dfrac{3}{14}$

(b) $\dfrac{3}{5}+\dfrac{2}{6}=\dfrac{18}{10}+\dfrac{10}{30}=\dfrac{28}{30}=\dfrac{14}{15}$

(c) $\dfrac{9}{11}-\dfrac{1}{3}=\dfrac{27}{33}-\dfrac{11}{33}=\dfrac{16}{33}$

(d) $\dfrac{3}{4}-\dfrac{1}{12}=\dfrac{9}{12}-\dfrac{1}{12}=\dfrac{8}{12}=\dfrac{2}{3}$

(e) $\dfrac{1}{5}\times\dfrac{3}{4}=\dfrac{3}{20}$

(f) $\dfrac{3}{10}\times\dfrac{1}{9}=\dfrac{3}{90}=\dfrac{1}{30}$

(g) $\dfrac{1}{9}\div\dfrac{2}{3}=\dfrac{1}{9}\times\dfrac{3}{2}=\dfrac{3}{18}=\dfrac{1}{6}$

(h) $\dfrac{4}{7}\div\dfrac{21}{24}=\dfrac{4}{7}\times\dfrac{24}{21}=\dfrac{96}{147}=\dfrac{32}{49}$

3. (a) $\dfrac{2}{5}=0.4=40\%$

(b) $\dfrac{6}{10}=0.6=60\%$

(c) $\dfrac{1}{8}=0.125=12.5\%$

4. (a) 10% of £68.00 is £6.80. Double that (to find 20%) is £13.60

(b) $75\%=\dfrac{3}{4}$

Find $\dfrac{1}{4}$ of $24:24\div4=6$

Find $\dfrac{3}{4}$ by multiplying by $3:6\times3=18$

Alternatively, find half, then half again and add the numbers:

50% + 25% = 75%

12 + 6 + 18

(c) 60% of 80

10% of 80 is 8

6 × 8 = 48

5. (a) $3x \geq 15$ (b) $-3x \geq 9$

          $x \geq \dfrac{15}{3}$ $x \leq \dfrac{9}{-3}$ (don't forget – dividing by a negative number reverses the inequality)

          $x \geq 5$ $x \leq -3$

  (c) $4x + 3 < 18$

     $4x \quad < 18 - 3$

     $4x \quad < 15$

     $x \quad < \dfrac{15}{4}$

     $x \quad < 3\dfrac{3}{4}$

6. (a) 3.0×10^2 (b) 3.28×10^5

  (c) 7.9428×10^3 (d) 2.59×10^{-1}

Chapter 4 – Mathematical language, reasoning and proof

1. (a) A quadrilateral can always be divided into two triangles, e.g.:

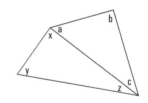

$$(\hat{a} + \hat{b} + \hat{c}) + (\hat{x} + \hat{y} + \hat{z}) = 180° + 180° = 360°$$

But, the four angles of the quadrilateral are also the sum of these six angles.

(b) Children could either draw several quadrilaterals, measure the angles and find the sum, or, tear off the corners and show they fit together to make one rotation.

2. (a) Our two even numbers can be written, 2a and 2b, where a and b are integers. Multiplying gives:

$$2a \times 2b = 2(2ab)$$

2ab is the product of three integers and must also be an integer (an assumption). Hence 2(2ab), the product of two even numbers, must be even.

(b) Writing our odd numbers as 2a + 1 and 2b + 1 and multiplying gives:

$$(2a+1)(2b+1) = 4ab + 2b + 2a + 1$$

The final unit makes it impossible to divide this expression by 2, so it is not even. Therefore, the product of two odd numbers is odd.

3. Three consecutive numbers must contain at least one even number of the form 2a, where a is an integer. The product of 2a and any other two integers gives a number divisible by 2, hence the product is always even.

4. Undertaken systematically, the possibilities are:

    abc bac cab

    acb bca cba

5. (a) $0.1 \times 60 = 6$ or $\frac{1}{2} \times 10 = 5$ would do.

    (b) This shape or variations on it would refute:

    (c) 8 and 6 are both factors of 24, but 8 is not a factor of 6 and 6 is not a factor of 8.

6. Assuming the truth of the theorem that the angle subtended at the centre is twice that at the circumference, we can argue:

    Let $\hat{x}$ be the angle AÔB, where O is the centre of the circle.

$$\text{Now } 2\hat{a} = \hat{x}$$

$$\text{and } 2\hat{b} = \hat{x}$$

$$\text{hence } 2\hat{a} = 2\hat{b}$$

$$\therefore \hat{a} = \hat{b}$$

7. Three standard methods of proof that could be used in primary schools are:

    • deductive proof;
    • disproof by counter-example;
    • proof by exhaustion.

8. The three ways in which we can represent mathematical ideas are:
   - language describing using words, phrases and sentences;
   - through the use of pictures/objects including number lines and mathematical apparatus;
   - using specialist symbols.

9. The following abbreviations mean:

   (a) OE Ordinary English;

   (b) ME Mathematical English.

10. Give three examples of each of the following:

    (a) Words that have the same meaning in ME and OE.

    (b) Words that have a different meaning in ME from OE.

    (c) Words that have an ME meaning only.

    Look back to the table in the section on Vocabulary to check your answers.

Chapter 5 – Algebra, equations, functions and graphs

1. (a) $5n^2 + 6n - n^2 + 4 - 2n + 1$

   $= 5n^2 - n^2 + 6n - 2n + 4 + 1$

   $= 4n^2 + 4n + 5$

   (b) $(pq)^2 + p^2q + 4p^2q^2 - 3p(qp) + pq^2$

   $= p^2q^2 + p^2q + 4p^2q^2 - 3pqp + pq^2$

   $= p^2q^2 + 4p^2q^2 + p^2q - 3ppq + pq^2$

   $= 5p^2q^2 - 2p^2q + pq^2$

2. a)

position	1	2	3	4	5
term	2	5	8	11	14

   3   3   3   3

   general term $3n - 1$

   (b)

position	1	2	3	4	5
term	4	8	12	16	20

   4   4   4   4

   general term $4n$

3. (a) a − 3b = 1   (1)

      a + 2b = 11   (2)

Subtracting equation (1) from equation (2) gives:

$a + 2b = 11$

$a - 3b = 1$

$\overline{\quad\quad 5b = 10}$

$b = 2$

Substituting for b in (2) gives:

a + 2b = 11

a + 4 = 11

a = 7

So a = 7 and b = 2

(b) 2a − 3b = 4   (1)

      a + 2b = 9   (2)

Multiplying equation (2) by 2 gives:

    2a + 4b =18   (3)

Subtracting equation (1) from equation (3) gives:

$2a + 4b = 18$

$2a - 3b = 4$

$\overline{\quad\quad 7b = 14}$

$b = 2$

So a = 5 and b =2

4. (a) 2y = 6x + 4

This needs to be expressed in the form y = mx + c. To do this, every term must be divided by 2, giving:

y = 3x + 2

So the gradient is 3 and the y-intercept is 2.

(b) x + 2y = 4

This is currently not of the form y = mx + c and therefore needs rearranging:

$x + 2y = 4$

$2y = 4 - x$

$2y = (-x) + 4$

$y = \dfrac{(-x)}{2} + 2$

So the gradient is $-\dfrac{1}{2}$ and the y intercept is 2.

5.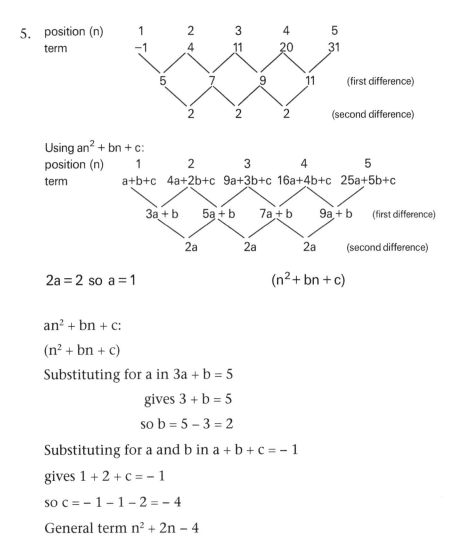

Using $an^2 + bn + c$:

position (n)	1	2	3	4	5
term	a+b+c	4a+2b+c	9a+3b+c	16a+4b+c	25a+5b+c

$2a = 2$ so $a = 1$ $(n^2 + bn + c)$

$an^2 + bn + c$:

$(n^2 + bn + c)$

Substituting for a in $3a + b = 5$

gives $3 + b = 5$

so $b = 5 - 3 = 2$

Substituting for a and b in $a + b + c = -1$

gives $1 + 2 + c = -1$

so $c = -1 - 1 - 2 = -4$

General term $n^2 + 2n - 4$

6. A conjecture is a hypothesis: something that has been surmised or deduced.

7. The methods that can be used to solve simultaneous linear equations are:

- 'trial and improvement' (or 'guess and check' but not 'trial and error' as this implies a mistake);
- eliminating the unknown by multiplying one of the equations to ensure that there is an equal number of a particular unknown in each equation;
- expressing one unknown in terms of another in one of the equations, then substituting the new expression into the other equation, which is then rearranged to find the solution.

8. A function is a rule that changes or maps one number onto another, often represented in primary schools as a 'function machine'.

Chapter 6 – Measures

1. 12 kg

2. 400 ml

3. The three important stages of development in children's understanding of measurement are:

   - direct comparison using matching, with no actual measuring;
   - using non-standard units;
   - using standard units.

4. The two different systems of units of measurement are Metric and Imperial.

5. SI stands for Système International.

6. The aspect of measurement that uses the same units in both systems is Time – seconds, minutes, hours.

7. Complete the following table to show the units of measurement:

	Metric	Imperial
Weight (mass)	g, kg, tonnes	ounces, pounds, stones, tons
Volume	cm³, m³	cubic inches/feet
Capacity	ml, cl, litres	fluid ounces, pints, gallons
Length	cm, m, km	inches, feet, yards, miles
Area	cm², m², hectares	square inches/feet/yards

8. Complete the following approximate equivalences:

Metric	Imperial
28 g	1 oz
1 kg	2.2 1b
16 cm³	1 cubic inch
1 m³	35 cubic feet
570 ml	1 pint
1 litre	1.75 pints
2.5 cm	1 inch
30 cm	1 foot
6.5 cm²	1 square inch
1 m²	11 square feet

9. The formulae give the volumes of the following regular 3-D shapes:

   a) $\frac{1}{3}\pi r^2 h$ cone

b) $\frac{1}{2}(1 \times b \times h)$ triangular prism

c) $1 \times b \times h$ cube/cuboid

d) $\pi r^2 h$ cylinder

10. Which formulae would you use to calculate the surface area of the following?

   a) A cube $6L^2$

   b) A circle πr^2

Chapter 7 – Geometry

1. square, rectangle, parallelogram, rhombus

2. 12 cm²

3. 23° 62° 87°, $\frac{1}{4}$ turn, 134°, 212°, $\frac{7}{8}$ of a turn (acute, acute, acute, right, obtuse, reflex, reflex)

4. 210 cm or 2.1 m

5. One possible answer for each is shown below:

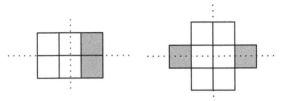

6. One possible answer for each is shown below:

7. (a) There are 35 hexominoes. (b) A regular hexahedron.

8. Thinking about 2-D shapes:

   (a) Types of triangle – equilateral, isosceles, scalene, right-angled (scalene or isosceles)

   (b) Types of quadrilateral – (any four from) square, rectangle, parallelogram, rhombus, kite, trapezium, isosceles trapezium

   (c) The four transformations that can be applied to 2-D shapes – translation, reflection, rotation and enlargement

9. In describing 3-D shapes:

(a) Face – the flat surface of a solid shape

(b) Edge – the line where two faces join

(c) Vertex – the point of intersection of edges

10. The following Cartesian co-ordinates would be in:

(a) (2, –6) the 4th quadrant

(b) (–4,7) the 2nd quadrant

(c) (2,4) the 1st quadrant

(d) (–3, –4) the 3rd quadrant

Chapter 8 – Statistics

1. (a) discrete (b) continuous (c) continuous (d) discrete

2. Nothing. Have you heard the saying, 'Lies, damned lies and statistics'? This is a good example of how data may have shown a correlation but in fact does not prove that babies are brought by storks! This is pure coincidence!

3. (a) Maths. Reasons for choice will vary, but may be based on answers (b) and (c).

(b) Maths: mean = 13.8   median = 14.5   mode = 12,18

English: mean = 12   median = 12.5   mode = 14

(c) Maths: range is between 5 and 20

interquartile range is between 10.5 and 17.5

English: range is between 3 and 19

interquartile range is between 9 and 15

(d) The only valid statement we can make is that the maths scores were higher than the English scores. It is impossible to tell from the data presented why this might be, but some possible reasons could be:

- the English test was harder than the maths test;
- the pupils are better at maths than they are at English;
- the English test was taken in poor conditions;
- some of the pupils cheated in the maths test!

4. (a) $\frac{1}{4}$ (b) $\frac{1}{6}$ (c) $\frac{1}{12}$ (d) 0

5. Four ways of displaying discrete data are (any four of) table, block graph, bar graph, bar-line graph, pie chart, scattergraph.

6. Four ways of displaying continuous data are scattergraph, line graph, frequency diagram, frequency histogram (possibly with a cumulative frequency diagram/curve).

7. Define the following terms:

   (a) Mean – the most common type of average; found by adding up all of the components in a set of data and dividing by the number of components in the set.

   (b) Median – the middle value in a set of data.

   (c) Mode – the value occurring most commonly in a set of data.

   (d) Range – a measure of the spread of a set of data: the interval between the least/greatest values.

   (e) Quartiles – another way of measuring a set of data: the lower quartile is the value one quarter of the way along a set of ordered data; the upper quartile is the value three quarters of the way along that set of ordered data.

8. The three possible ways of identifying the probability of an event are:

   - working from prior knowledge, e.g. as in weather forecasting;
   - experimental probability – using the findings from repeating an experiment;
   - theoretical probability – using theoretical knowledge of the situation.

Glossary

abscissa   the first number in a pair of Cartesian co-ordinates. The abscissa always represents the distance along the x-axis.

angle   a measurement of turn.

approximation   an inexact result adequate and appropriate for a given purpose.

arc   a curved line that forms part of the circumference of a circle.

associative law   numbers can be regrouped to simplify a question while making no difference to the answer. It is true for addition and multiplication:

$$(a + b) + c = a + (b + c) \qquad\qquad (a \times b) \times c = a \times (b \times c)$$

average   the general term used for using one number to represent a set of data.

bar graph   a graph that uses bars to represent data.

bar-line graph   a graph that uses lines to represent data.

block graph   a graph used to display discrete data where one block can represent one or many item(s) of data.

BODMAS   the order of precedence given to the operations when working out complex expressions. It stands for:

B – brackets
O – of
D – division
M – multiplication
A – addition
S – subtraction

Could also be BIDMAS where the 'I' represents indices.

box and whisker plot a graphical representation that allows for comparison of two sets of data.

capacity how much liquid volume a container can hold when full.

Cartesian co-ordinates a pair of numbers that locate a point on a plane with reference to two axes (can also refer to three axes in order to locate a point in three dimensions).

chord a straight line connecting any two points on a curve. When a chord passes through the centre of a circle it is called the diameter.

column value the value of a digit defined by its position in a number.

commutative law: the order in which the operation is performed makes no difference to the answer. It is true for addition and multiplication:

$$a + b = b + a \qquad a \times b = b \times a$$

congruence shapes are said to be congruent if they are the same shape and size.

conjecture a hypothesis, something that has been surmised or deduced.

conservation understanding that the quantity of matter remains unchanged regardless of its arrangement.

continuous data data that is measured. Every item of data can be placed along a continuum, for example, lengths of leaves.

counter-example disproving an assertion by finding an exception.

cumulative frequency a table displaying the running total of a set of data.

cumulative frequency curve a graph of the running total of a set of data.

data a set of facts, numbers or information.

decimal a fractional number expressed using places to the right of the decimal point.

deduction a conclusion based on a set of true statements.

denominator   the bottom number in a fraction, representing the number of fractional parts the unit has been divided into.

discrete data   data that can be counted. Every item of data can be placed in a category, for example, colours of cars.

distributive law   one operation is 'distributed out' over another operation. It is true for multiplication over addition and multiplication over subtraction:

$$a \times (b + c) = (a \times b) + (a \times c) \qquad a \times (b - c) = (a \times b) - (a \times c)$$

It is also true that division is 'right distributive' over addition and subtraction (i.e. the division needs to be on the right side of the brackets):

$$(a + b) \div c = (a \div c) + (b \div c) \qquad (a - b) \div c = (a \div c) - (b \div c)$$

dividend   within the operation of division, the number that is divided by another number.

divisor   within the operation of division, the number that divides another number.

edge   the line where two faces join (i.e. the intersection of two plane faces of a solid).

enlargement   each measurement is multiplied by a scale factor in order to enlarge or reduce an image.

equation   a statement that two expressions are equal.

estimation   the rough answer (a judgement of an approximate value or amount).

exhaustion   a proof that is arrived at by considering all possibilities.

experimental probability   the number between 0 and 1 that is found by dividing the number of outcomes by the total number of trials.

expression   a general term used to describe mathematical terms.

face   the flat surface of a solid shape (i.e. parts of planes).

factor   a number that divides another number exactly, for example 8 is a factor of 32, but 5 is not.

fraction   a fraction is expressed as the quotient of two numbers, the dividend is the numerator, the divisor the denominator.

frequency diagram   a table displaying continuous data grouped into classes.

frequency histogram   a graph displaying continuous data grouped into classes.

function   a rule that changes or maps one number on to another.

gradient   the slope of a graph.

imperial measure   introduced in the Magna Carta in 1215, for example, pints, gallons, miles, etc.

independent events   events when the outcome of one event does not affect the outcome of another event, for example, flipping two coins.

index form (or index notation)   a concise way of writing repeated multiplication of a number by itself, for example, $10 \times 10 \times 10 \times 10 = 10^4$.

inequality   a statement that one quantity is greater or less than another.

integer   a whole number (not a fractional number), for example, 2, 57 and 389. Examples of non-integers are 1.2 and 0.5.

interquartile range   the interval between the upper quartile and the lower quartile in a set of data.

irrational numbers   the set of numbers that cannot be expressed in fractional form.

inverse   in mathematics inverse means 'opposite'. Thus, addition is the inverse of subtraction.

line graph   a graph used to display continuous data, where curves or line segments join points of measured data.

linear equation   takes the form $ay + bx + c = 0$. A linear equation can always be represented as a straight line graph.

lower quartile   the value one quarter of the way along a set of ordered data.

mass   the amount of matter contained in an object.

mean   the sum of the values in a set of data divided by the total number of items in that set.

median   the middle value of a set of ordered data.

minuend   the quantity from which another quantity is to be subtracted.

mode   the value that occurs most often in a set of data.

mutually exclusive events   events which, having happened, exclude any other outcome from occurring in that same event, for example, throwing a 3 on a die excludes a 1, 2, 4, 5 or 6 being thrown at the same time.

net   a flat shape that can be folded to form a solid.

numerator   the top number in a fraction representing the number of fractional parts.

ordering   putting a collection of items in order from smallest to biggest/biggest to smallest according to weight, length, thickness, etc.

ordinate   the second number in a pair of Cartesian co-ordinates. The ordinate always represents the distance along the y-axis.

parallel   lines travelling in the same direction but which will never meet.

percentage   fractions with a denominator of 100. They can also be represented as decimals, for example $\dfrac{1}{4} = \dfrac{25}{100} = 0.25 = 25\%$

perpendicular   two lines are said to be perpendicular if they meet at right angles.

pi (π)   an irrational number found when the circumference of a circle is divided by the diameter. It is approximately equal to 3.141592...

pictogram   a form to display discrete data where one picture/symbol can represent one or many item(s) of data.

pie chart   a circle graph cut into sectors.

place value   place value is used by number systems that allow the same digit to carry different values based on its position.

Platonic solids   the five regular polyhedra, comprising the regular tetrahedron, the cube, the regular octahedron, the regular dodecahedron and the regular icosahedron.

polygon   a plane shape with straight sides and many angles.

polyhedron (pl. polyhedra)   a solid formed from many flat faces.

prism   a solid shape with a uniform cross section.

probability   used to measure the likelihood of certain events occurring in the future.

probability scale   a scale from 0 to 1 that is used to measure the likelihood of an event occurring, with 0 being impossible and 1 being certain.

proportion   compares part of a quantity with the whole, for example, a ratio of 1:3 results in proportions of 1 out of 4 and 3 out of 4.

pyramid   a solid that has a polygon base and all other faces triangular.

quantity value   the value you assign to a digit when you have established its column value.

quotient   the result when one number is divided by another number.

range   the interval between the greatest and least values in a set of data.

ratio   a comparison between two quantities.

rational numbers   the set of all numbers that can be written as fractions.

real numbers   the set of rational numbers and irrational numbers combined.

recurring decimal   a fraction in which a figure or a group of figures reoccur indefinitely, for example, 3.33333 or 2.14514145, etc.

reduction   combining different parts of an equation to make it simpler.

reflection   when a shape is reflected, a mirror image is created. The shape and size remain unchanged and the two images are congruent.

reflective symmetry   also sometimes called line symmetry. A shape is said to have reflective symmetry if it can be folded so that one half fits exactly on top of the other half.

restoration   simplifying an equation by performing the same operation on each side.

rotation   rotation involves a turn around a fixed point. The shape and size remain unchanged, the two images are congruent.

rotational symmetry   a shape is said to have rotational symmetry if it looks the same in different positions when rotated about its centre.

scattergraph   a graph representing two types of data plotted as co-ordinates.

sector   a wedge from a circle (like a slice of pie).

sigma   means 'the sum of'. The symbol for sigma is Σ.

similarity   shapes are said to be similar if all the angles are the same size and the shapes are the same but of different size, i.e. one is an enlargement of the other.

simultaneous linear equations   two linear equations which have a common solution.

square number   the number we get by multiplying an integer by itself.

standard form   sometimes called standard index form as it uses powers of 10, i.e. 10 expressed in index form. It is a shorthand way of writing very small and very large numbers that would require a huge number of digits if written in full.

statistics   statistics help us to bring order to data and to draw information from it.

subtrahend   the number or term to be subtracted.

Système International (S.I.)   determines the units of measurement used in the metric system, for example, millimetres, kilograms, litres, etc.

terms   algebraic quantities that are separated from each other in expressions by operations.

theoretical probability   the number between 0 and 1 that is found by dividing the number of actual outcomes by the total number of possible outcomes.

transitivity   a mathematical relationship used to compare two objects or events, for example, if A is shorter than B, and B is shorter than C, then A must be shorter than C.

translation   this takes place when a shape is moved from one place to another just by sliding it (without rotating, reflecting or enlarging).

upper quartile   the value three-quarters of the way along a set of ordered data.

vertex   the point of intersection of edges.

volume   the amount of three-dimensional space an object occupies.

vulgar fraction   a fraction expressed by numerator and denominator, not decimally; used in ordinary calculations (the original meaning of the word 'vulgar' was 'as used by ordinary people').

weight   the force exerted on a body due to gravity.

y-intercept   the point at which a graph crosses the y-axis.

References

ACME (2012) *Response to the Draft Primary National Curriculum for Mathematics.* Available at http://www.acme-uk.org/media/10025/20120807%20-%20acme%20 ncr%20response%20part%20a%20%20final.pdf (accessed 15/10/17).

Anghileri, J. (2006) *Teaching Number Sense*, 2nd edn. London: Continuum.

Appel, K. and Haken, W. (1976) Every Planar Map is Four Colorable. *Bulletin of the American Mathematical Society*, 82(5): 711–12. Available at http://projecteuclid.org/ euclid.bams/1183538218 (accessed 15/10/17).

Askew, W. and Wiliam, D. (1995) *Recent Research in Mathematics Education 5–16.* London: Ofsted.

Atiyah, M. (2001) Mathematics in the 20th Century: Geometry versus Algebra. *Mathematics Today*, 37(2): 46–53.

Ball, D. L. and Bass, H. (2000) Interweaving Content and Pedagogy in Teaching and Learning to Teach: Knowing and Using Mathematics in Boaler, J. (ed) *Multiple Perspectives in the Teaching and Learning of Mathematics*. Westport: Ablex, pp. 83–104.

Bew, P. (2011) *Independent Review of Key Stage 2 Testing, Assessment and Accountability: Final Report.* London: DfE.

Boulton-Lewis, G., Wilss, G. M. and Mutch, S. L. (1996) An Analysis of Young Children's Strategies and Use of Devices of Length Measurement. *Journal of Mathematical Behaviour*, 15: 329–47.

Carpenter, T. P. and Levi, L. (2000) *Developing Conceptions of Algebraic Reasoning in the Primary Grades: Research Report.* National Center for Improving Student Learning and Achievement in Mathematics and Science, University of Wisconsin-Madison, October, Report No. 00-2. Available at https://eric.ed.gov/?id=ED470471 (accessed 15/10/17).

Carraher, D., Schliemann, A., Brizuela, B. and Earnest, D. (2006) Arithmetic and Algebra in Early Mathematics Education. *Journal for Research in Mathematics Education*, 37(2): 87–115.

Charalambous, C. Y., Hill, H. C. and Ball, D. L. (2011) Prospective Teachers' Learning to Provide Instructional Explanations: How Does It Look and What Might It Take? *Journal of Mathematics Teacher Education*, 14(6) 441–3.

Clements, D. H., Battista, M. T., Sarama, J., Swaminathan, S. and McMillen, S. (1997) Students' Development of Length Measurement Concepts in a Logo-based Unit on Geometric Paths. *Journal for Research in Mathematics Education*, 28(1): 70–95.

Clements, D. H. and Stephan, M. (2003) Measurement in Pre-K to Grade 2 Mathematics in Clements, D. H., Sarama, J. and DiBiase, A. (eds) *Engaging Young Children in Mathematics*. London: Routledge.

DfE (2011a) *The Framework for the National Curriculum*. A Report by the Expert Panel for the National Curriculum Review. London: DfE.

DfE (2011b) *Independent Review of Key Stage 2 Testing, Assessment and Accountability: Government Response*. London: DfE.

DfE (2011c) *Teachers' Standards*. London: DfE. Available at https://www.gov.uk/government/uploads/system/uploads/attachment_data/file/301107/Teachers__Standards.pdf (accessed 15/10/17).

DfE (2013a) *Primary Assessment and Accountability under the New National Curriculum*. London: DfE. Available at https://www.gov.uk/government/uploads/system/uploads/attachment_data/file/245919/Primary_assessment_and_accountability_under_the_new_curriculum_consultation_document.pdf (accessed 15/10/17).

DfE (2013b) *National Curriculum in England: Mathematics Programmes of Study – Key Stages 1 and 2*. London: DfE. Available at: https://www.gov.uk/government/uploads/system/uploads/attachment_data/file/239129/PRIMARY_National_Curriculum_-_Mathematics.pdf (accessed 1/10/2017).

DfE (2017a) *Statutory Framework for the Early Years Foundation Stage: Setting the Standards for Learning, Development and Care for Children from Birth to Five*. London: DfE. Available at https://www.gov.uk/government/publications/early-years-foundation-stage-framework--2 (accessed 15/10/17).

DfE (2017b) *Primary Assessment in England Government: Consultation Response*. London: DfE. Available at https://www.gov.uk/government/uploads/system/uploads/attachment_data/file/644871/Primary_assessment_consultation_response.pdf (accessed 15/10/17).

Fyhn, A. (2008) A Climbing Class' Reinvention of Angles. *Educational Studies in Mathematics*, 67(1): 19–35.

Gray, E. and Tall, D. (2001) Relationships Between Embodied Objects and Symbolic Procepts: An Explanatory Theory of Success and Failure in Mathematics. *Proceedings of the 25th Conference of the International Group for the Psychology of Mathematics Education*. Utrecht: Freudenthal Institute, Utrecht University, pp. 65–72.

Gray, E. (2008) Compressing the Counting Process: Strength from the Flexible Interpretation of Symbols in Thompson, I. (ed.) *Teaching and Learning Early Number*. Maidenhead: Open University Press.

Jones, I. (2008) A Diagrammatic View of the Equals Sign: Arithmetical Equivalence as a Means, not an End. *Research in Mathematics Education*, 10(2): 151–65.

Jones, K. and Mooney, C. (2003) Making Space for Geometry in Thompson, I. (ed.) *Enhancing Primary Mathematics Teaching*. Maidenhead: Open University Press, pp. 3–15.

Kieren, T. E. (1976) On the Mathematical, Cognitive, and Instructional Foundations of Rational Numbers in Lesh, R. A. and Brandberd, D. A. (eds) *Number and Measurement*. Columbus, Ohio: ERIC/SMEAC.

Littleton, K., Mercer, N., Dawes, L., Wegerif, R., Rowe, D. and Sams, C. (2005) Talking and Thinking Together at Key Stage 1. *Early Years*, 25(2): 167–82.

Ma, L. (1999) *Knowing and Teaching Elementary Mathematics*. New Jersey: Lawrence Erlbaum.

McNeil, N. and Alibali, M. (2005) Why Won't You Change Your Mind? Knowledge of Operational Patterns Hinders Learning and Performance on Equations. *Child Development*, 76: 883–99.

Mercer, N. and Sams, C. (2006a) The Analysis of Classroom Talk: Methods and Methodologies.

British Journal of Educational Psychology, 80(1): 1–14.

Mercer, N. and Sams, C. (2006b) Teaching Children How to Use Language to Solve Maths Problems. *Language and Education: An International Journal*, 20(6): 507–28.

Molina, M., Castro, E. and Mason, J. (2008) Elementary School Students' Approaches to Solving True/False Number Sentences. *PNA: Revista de Investigación en Didáctica de la Matemática*, 2: 75–86.

Mooney, C., Briggs, M., Fletcher, M., Hansen, A. and McCulloch, J. (2018) *Primary Mathematics: Teaching Theory and Practice*, 8th edn. London: Learning Matters.

Morris, H. (2001) Issues Raised by Testing Trainee Primary Teachers' Mathematical Knowledge. *Mathematics Education Research Journal*, 3: 37–47.

Nunes, T., Schliemann, A. D. and Carraher, D. W. (1993) *Street Mathematics and School Mathematics*. Cambridge: Cambridge University Press.

Price, R. and Raiker, A. (2003) Is Teacher Confidence a Factor in the Effective Teaching of Datahandling? *Topic*, 29: 7–11.

Rowland, T., Martin, S., Barber, P. and Heal, C. (2001) Investigating the Mathematics Subject Matter Knowledge of Pre-service Elementary School Teachers in van den Heuvel-Panhuizen, M. (ed.) *Proceedings of the 23rd Conference of the International Group for the Psychology of Mathematics Education*. Utrecht: Freudenthal Institute, Utrecht University, vol. 4, pp. 121–8.

Straker, A. (1993) *Talking Points in Mathematics*. Cambridge: Cambridge University Press.

TDA (2007) *Professional Standards for Teachers: Qualified Teacher Status*. London: TDA.

Thomas, M. and Tall, D. (2001) The Long-term Cognitive Development of Symbolic Algebra in Chick, H., Stacey, K. and Vincent, J. (eds), *12th ICMI Study Conference: The Future of the Teaching and Learning of Algebra*. Melbourne: University of Melbourne, pp. 590–7.

Thompson, I. (ed.) (1997) *Teaching and Learning Early Number*. Buckingham: Open University Press.

Thompson, I. (2009) Place Value? *Mathematics Teaching*, 215: 4–5.

Thompson, I. and Bramald, R. (2002) *An Investigation of the Relationship Between Young Children's Understanding of Place Value and their Competence at Mental Addition*. Final report submitted to the Nuffield Foundation. Newcastle: Department of Education, University of Newcastle upon Tyne.

Tickell, C. (2011) *The Early Years: Foundations for Life, Health and Learning*. An Independent Report on the Early Years Foundation Stage to Her Majesty's Government. London: DfE.

Whiteley, W. (2004) *Visualization in Mathematics: Claims and Questions towards a Research Program*. Toronto: York University. Available at: http://www.math.yorku.ca/~whiteley/Visualization.pdf (accessed 15/10/17).

Williams, P. (2008) *Independent Review of Mathematics Teaching in Early Years Settings and Primary Schools*. London: DCSF. Available at: http://dera.ioe.ac.uk/8365/7/Williams%20Mathematics_Redacted.pdf (accessed 15/10/17).

Witt, M. (2014) *Primary Mathematics for Trainee Teachers*. London: SAGE.

Index